Betty Falk has been a supporter of SHELTER from its beginnings, though she considers it a national disgrace that there is any need for such an organization in the British Isles. She was the founder and first Chairman of Reigate and Redhill Shelter Group, one of the first of the three hundred groups now in operation throughout Great Britain. 'In 1967, we formed what must have been in its early days about the most unorthodox committee ever, but after grinding slowly, painfully and sometimes hilariously into gear, we eventually got a hard-working and pretty successful group going.'

Mrs Falk is the author of *The Peacock Cookery Book*. As a change from committee work, she decided to put her interest in cookery to account on SHELTER's behalf by collecting, with the help of the group, and editing for publication the recipes in this book.

THE
SHELTER
COOKERY
BOOK

Edited by Betty Falk

Illustrated by
Michael Spink

Penguin Books

Penguin Books Ltd, Harmondsworth,
Middlesex, England
Penguin Books Inc., 7110 Ambassador Road,
Baltimore, Maryland 21207, U.S.A.
Penguin Books Australia Ltd, Ringwood,
Victoria, Australia

First published 1971
Copyright © SHELTER, 1971

Made and printed in Great Britain by
Richard Clay (The Chaucer Press) Ltd, Bungay, Suffolk
Set in Monotype Plantin

CONTENTS

6 *Contents*

8 *Contents*

POULTRY AND MEAT

VEGETABLE DISHES

PUDDINGS AND SWEET DISHES

CAKES

MISCELLANEOUS

FOREWORD

In the four years during which I was working full-time for SHELTER, I went to a lot of places for the homeless: speaking at public meetings; appearing on television; writing in the columns of national newspapers. Even so, being perched precariously before the pâté, paella, and prune bombe in a cookery book is certainly a new experience.

Far be it from me in these few words, therefore, to attempt to teach grandmother to suck, boil, poach or scramble eggs. It just isn't my subject.

But homelessness is.

I have personally visited many of the families who eke out an existence in slums today. I have met a family in north London, for instance, which – apart from being crammed into two damp rooms – has to share a cold water tap and sparse cooking facilities with two other families in the same house. Moving east across the city, I can tell of a family living in a tenement block whose kitchen was barely large enough for one person to turn around in, and which had bugs crawling out of large cracks in the crumbling walls, and two large – and regularly used – rat holes under the sink.

In Birmingham I have met a hard-tried mother who, after a day's work, has to return home and attempt to cook a decent meal for a family of five on nothing more than a primus stove.

Faced by such cases, SHELTER has always been fortunate in being able to call upon the valuable support of people from all walks of life. It is one such supporter who has worked to create this book. To her I give my thanks, and also to all the contributors to this book who have taken the trouble to send a recipe as a gesture of support for the work SHELTER is doing. But it is the three million families living in appalling and overcrowded conditions in this country who made the venture necessary. SHELTER alone cannot solve their problems. The answer lies with you: your attitudes; your understanding; your support.

Des Wilson

INTRODUCTION

Some of the people who have been kind enough to send one of their favourite recipes for this book – and a surprising number of them are men – are evidently keen and accomplished cooks. Others simply consider food as fuel and have obviously had to rack their brains or those of their wives, girl-friends or house-keepers to produce some kind of recipe for something they like to eat. And some just enjoy good food and hasten to make it quite clear that they would not personally dream of so much as picking up a wooden spoon let alone actually cooking anything.

In the numerous cases where women have done the work and sent a recipe on behalf of a distinguished husband, lover or em-ployer while themselves remaining anonymous, I thank them very much. I wish I could mention cases where men have sent recipes on behalf of famous wives or girl-friends but I don't actually know of any in this book which come into this category though considering the increasing number of men who cook well and enthusiastically there is no reason why this should not be so.

Anyway, I think – and I trust the people who buy this book will agree – the result is an amusing and heterogeneous collection of splendid recipes for many different kinds of dishes, some sophisticated and some extremely simple. I have personally had a great deal of entertainment in compiling the book from comparing the choice of recipe with the image presented to the world by the contributor – and I hope readers will enjoy this game too.

I also asked people to say how they wished to be described. Many failed to do this, either out of modesty or by oversight or perhaps they just couldn't think of a suitable description of their own activities. In these cases, in order to preserve the pattern, I have done my best with the help of advice from friends, *Who's Who* and other reference books to pin some kind of label on them and I hope they will forgive me if they find the designations unsuitable.

I have taken an editor's privilege of putting all the recipes into a more or less standardized form for clarity's sake while retaining as much of the original wording in which they were sent to me as possible; of clarifying where instructions seemed confused or even downright impossible (but in the latter case, I have tried to check with the contributor before making a change, especially where he or she was evidently a dedicated cook or eater).

Many good wishes for the success of the work that SHELTER is doing came with the recipes and the warm response of a high percentage of people approached for a contribution has been most rewarding. In thanking them once again I have only one more request to make. Please try to persuade your friends to buy as many copies as possible, for SHELTER's sake.

Betty Falk

ABOUT SHELTER

At the time of going to press there are approximately three million families in Britain who the authorities say are living in slums, near-slums or grossly overcrowded conditions. Of these, SHELTER would argue that one million are living in the worst slums. This is over and above the 4,117 families (20,820 men, women and children) living in hostels for the homeless on any one night last year, though only one in four seeking temporary accommodation is admitted; and it does not include the unknown numbers of people who are sleeping rough or in cars.

These families can only face heart-break and despair, knowing that they cannot give their children a fair chance in life. At best they are cramped and overcrowded, with all that this entails, unable to get proper sleep at night, their nerves on edge during the day as children play and quarrel in the restricted space in which everything else must also be done.

Slum houses can be death traps. It may be dangerous to boil water in an overcrowded kitchen, but mothers have no choice when they have no hot tap. It may be dangerous to have a paraffin stove where children are playing and where washing is drying, but many families cannot afford electricity or gas. Disease is another constant hazard where walls run with water or where families are obliged to share their lavatory with up to twelve others, none of whom are responsible for cleaning them.

SHELTER National Campaign for the Homeless exists to help families like these whom we consider homeless. SHELTER was set up late in 1966 by a number of individuals and organizations within the voluntary housing movement. The organizations were the Notting Hill Housing Trust, the Catholic Housing Aid Society, the National Federation of Housing Societies (through its Housing Societies Charitable Trust), Christian Action and the British Churches Housing Trust. Des Wilson, then a young journalist and publicity adviser, became the Campaign's first full-time worker and was involved in the initial research and forward planning for the Campaign's launch. He became the first Campaign Director, and in May 1967, the first Director. He was succeeded as Director in January 1971 by John Willis who had previously been Housing Director. Des Wilson retains his involvement with SHELTER as a trustee.

A large proportion of SHELTER's money has been raised through the 273 Groups throughout the country. These are made up of people who are deeply concerned about the housing situation and who, as well as raising large sums of money, try to keep tabs on the local housing situation.

SHELTER works through local housing associations who are able to increase the value of the money SHELTER gives them between six and eight times, by using it with local government loans and grants. The housing associations buy up properties and convert them into flats which can be let at cost rent to families who were previously homeless. By working in this way, SHELTER can rehouse a family for £325 and is now rehousing families at a rate of ten families per day.

SHELTER allocates a proportion of its income to housing experiments. Housing renewal projects have been set up in Bradford and Liverpool 8, and a housing aid service has been established in London. SNAP, the SHELTER Neighbourhood Action Project, in Liverpool, aims to involve local residents from about 740 houses in improving both their homes and their environment generally. With an architect/town planner as Director and tremendous local enthusiasm, this project has got off to a great start. The Bradford scheme, SHARE (SHELTER Housing and

Renewal Experiment), still in its early stages, is a most exciting urban renewal project aimed at improving race relations through housing. SHAC (SHELTER (Family) Housing Aid Centre) is in London. It incorporates a number of schemes such as an Out of London Scheme, through which families wishing to move out of London to obtain adequate housing are helped to find accommodation and jobs in towns like Halifax. There's a special unit which aims to help fatherless families and an Emergency Department which keeps track of the number of spare beds throughout London for really desperate families. Families can receive general housing advice, particularly information about obtaining mortgages, from SHAC. Similar housing advisory centres are being set up in Glasgow and Edinburgh.

7½ per cent of SHELTER's total funds are spent on education. This includes 'pressure' activities – trying to persuade Government and local authorities to devote more money to housing, publishing reports revealing the extent of the housing problem and its effects, particularly on children. It also includes education about housing – informing young couples through booklets like *A Home of Your Own* how to start buying a house. SHELTER's Youth Department hopes to introduce housing education into the school syllabus, and employs two Youth Organizers to tour the country, speaking to school-children about the housing situation. For SHELTER believes that it is only when the full extent of the problem of homelessness is realized, and its effects recognized, that the necessary money will be poured into housing by the Government. In the meantime, SHELTER exists as a highly necessary rescue service and pressure group.

HORS D'OEUVRE

from Richard Lester, Film Director

Anchoïade

I have chosen Anchoïade because it is the fastest hors d'œuvre I know to prepare, and life is like that.

To serve a variable number, according to the size they are cut

2 tins anchovies
milk
olive oil
2 cloves garlic
wine vinegar

2 tablesp. breadcrumbs
1 teasp. paprika
slices of bread with crusts
  removed

Soak contents of 2 tins of anchovies in warm milk to reduce their salt content. It is useful if they can soak for a few hours, but not essential. Place the anchovies in a food mincer or blender, or failing that use a mortar and pestle, or failing that hit them hard with a firm object. As you do this, gradually add enough olive oil to make the final concoction the consistency of beaten cream. At the same time add 2 finely chopped garlic cloves, 2 tablesp. breadcrumbs and 1 teasp. paprika. If you have a blender everything can be thrown in together, without any preparation (garlic cloves, crusts of bread, etc.) so in fact there is only 30 seconds of preparation.

    Toast crustless bread slices on one side only; spread the mixture on the untoasted side, sprinkle with 1 teasp. wine vinegar for each slice and brown hard under the grill. Serve as an hors d'œuvre or with drinks before a meal.

from Silvino Trompetto, Maître Chef des Cuisines, Savoy Restaurant

L'ananas au crabe à l'américaine

To serve 8

4 very small pineapples
8 tablesp. crab meat
1 teasp. chopped chives
½ green pepper, chopped
pinch paprika

4 anchovy fillets, chopped
¼ pt double cream
2 dessertsp. mayonnaise
4 tomatoes, sliced in 4 and pips removed

Cut pineapples in half lengthways, scoop out flesh and cut into small dice. Mix pineapple, crab meat, chives, pepper, paprika and anchovies (which should be very salted ones) with the cream and mayonnaise. Do this very gently but thoroughly, and add a little salt. Dress the mixture in the pineapple shells and decorate with tomato slices. Serve chilled.

(Ed: Mr Trompetto invented this recipe specially for us. He says it may be prepared in the morning for the evening.)

from Christopher Fry, Dramatist

Bimbo's special

To serve 4

1 tin Campbell's consommé
2 pckts Philadelphia cream cheese

1 teasp. yellow curry powder
dash of sherry (optional)

Put half the consommé and all the other ingredients into a blender and blend until smooth. Pour this mixture into individual soup bowls; heat the rest of the consommé and pour over. Chill and decorate with bits of greenery.

from Noel Streatfeild, Author
Curry eggs

To serve 8

4 hard-boiled eggs
1 large size Primula cheese
1 dessertsp. curry powder

1 large size tin Crosse and Black-
    well's consommé
fresh or dried herbs to taste

Mash eggs and cheese together, adding curry powder. Heat half
the consommé and pour over mixture. Leave to get cold. The
other half of the consommé should be melted only and not
allowed to get warm, then poured over the rest. Pour the mixture
into 8 small dishes, sprinkle with a few chopped or rubbed
herbs and chill.

from the Rt Rev. G. E. Reindorp, Bishop of Guildford
Chicken liver pâté

1 packet of chicken livers (about
    6)
6 slices streaky bacon
½ oz. butter
1 clove garlic

1 large slice of green pepper
cream off top of the milk (about
    a cup full)
1 egg

Chop bacon roughly and cook gently with livers in the butter
until soft, then put all ingredients except egg into liquidizer
and reduce to pulp. Add egg and mix again in liquidizer.

Cook as for an egg custard (i.e. standing in a dish of water) for 30–35 minutes. When cooked, pour on enough melted butter to cover the top. Cool fast and keep in fridge.

from Rumer Godden, Author
Liver pâté

This recipe for an inexpensive pâté while as full of taste as any exotic pâté maison, has simple ingredients and goes far when served with hot toast on which to spread it. Butter on the toast is not needed.

4 oz. cooked liver (fried with an onion) (Ed. suggests ox or pig liver)	1 onion, very finely chopped (or minced with meats)
3 rashers streaky bacon	¼ teasp. mace
2 oz. chopped cooked ham or a 2 oz. tin chopped Danish ham	salt and pepper
	chopped parsley
	1 large or 2 small eggs

Mince liver, bacon, ham (and onion if wished) three times; each time the mixture goes through the mincer it will get more pâté-like. Put mixture in pudding basin and beat in seasoning, onion (if not minced with meats) and parsley. Beat egg/eggs and add to mixture. Beat all together until smooth. Taste and adjust seasoning. Put mixture into well-oiled pâté mould or small fire-proof dish, cover with foil and bake in bain-marie in a *very* slow oven for one hour. Serve cold.

from Michael Geliot, Opera and Theatre Director
Pâté

This is a very easy version to make and it looks very beautiful when turned out because of the marbled appearance of the bacon.

1 slice white bread	6 oz. pig's or calf's liver, minced or chopped fine
milk	

6 oz. sausage meat	1 large egg
2 shallots or half an onion, chopped	pepper
	brandy (optional)
1 tablesp. chopped parsley	rindless streaky bacon
1 clove garlic, crushed	

Heat the bread with enough milk for it to become soft. Add this to all the other ingredients except for the streaky bacon. You may add brandy if you can spare it. Mix the ingredients very thoroughly or pass them through a not too fine Mouli. The mixture should be fairly moist. Turn into a terrine or a deep dish lined with the bacon. Cover with a lid with a small hole, or with foil with a small slit in it. Place in a bain-marie and cook in a moderate oven until it is brown on the outside but still pink inside (about 1 hour). It can be cooked, covered, in a pressure cooker for 15 minutes.

When slightly cool, remove lid and place a heavy weight on top (a heavy jug of water will do). Leave overnight. Then cover and keep in fridge until needed. (It will keep for about a week in a fridge.)

Remove from fridge before serving and place dish in hot water for a moment. Then turn out. Serve as an hors d'œuvre with toast or else, thickly sliced, as a main course with salad.

from Peter Hall, Film, Theatre and Opera Director
Cod's roe pâté

To serve 4

| 4 oz. smoked cod's roe | 1 small onion finely grated |
| 4 oz. Philadelphia cream cheese | juice of ½ lemon |

Scrape roe from skin if using fresh, or turn from pot into a basin of hot water and leave for five minutes to remove some of the salt. Drain on absorbent kitchen paper. Put into a basin with cheese and onion and, using a wooden spoon, mix to a creamy consistency, gradually adding lemon juice. Pile into a small bowl and garnish with parsley. Serve with fresh crusty bread and a bowl of black olives.

from Lady Isobel Barnett, Radio and Television Personality

Marjorie's pâté dish

A quick, easy dish which will do either as an hors d'œuvre or as a main dish for a cold lunch.

To serve 4

any kind of pâté preferred – about ½ lb.
5 hard-boiled eggs

1 large tin Campbell's consommé
¼ pt cream
1 tablesp. sherry

Cover the bottom of a shallow dish, pint size or larger, with the pâté. Save a little of the consommé to decorate the top of the dish with jelly, and put the rest in liquidizer with eggs. Mix. Add cream and sherry. Mix again. Pour over pâté. Garnish and chill.

from Sir Michael Redgrave, Actor

Fonds d'artichauts au gratin

tinned artichoke hearts (1 or 2 per person)
cheese sauce

chopped cooked ham
a little grated Parmesan cheese
paprika

For each person, put one or two tinned artichoke hearts into a fireproof ramekin, cover with cheese sauce into which a little chopped, cooked ham has been stirred, sprinkle with Parmesan cheese and brown under the grill. Decorate with a pinch of paprika before serving.

from Mollie Lee, Editor of Woman's Hour

Mushroom hors d'œuvre

To serve 4

½lb. button mushrooms whole (or if large, cut in half)

2 tablesp. water
2 tablesp. olive oil

2 tablesp. dry white wine
1 tablesp. lemon juice
bouquet garni and a little extra
   parsley

pepper and salt
1 dessertsp. tomato purée
   (optional)

Wash and prepare mushrooms. Simmer together water, oil, wine, lemon juice, bouquet garni and seasoning for 5 minutes. Put in mushrooms and simmer for a further 5 minutes or so (with tomato purée if liked). Leave to get thoroughly cold in fridge. Serve in glass dish scattered with a little chopped parsley.

from John Schlesinger, Film Director

Taramasalata

I first discovered taramasalata when I went to Greece to make a documentary on *The Guns of Navarone* and my interpreter gave me the recipe.

To serve 4

3–4 slices white bread
½ lb. smoked cod's roe
½ large onion

1–2 cloves garlic
½ pt olive oil
juice of 1–2 lemons

Soak the bread in water and squeeze out the liquid with your hands. Remove the roe from the skin by scraping away with a spoon. Mix the roe and the bread together in a large basin (you need about twice as much roe as bread) and add the onion and garlic finely chopped.

Using a wire whisk, gradually add the oil, beating fiercely, and when the mixture gets too thick, thin out with the lemon juice. Taste as you go along, adding more oil or lemon juice as necessary. Serve with black olives and either hot toast or black bread.

N.B. Don't use the blender as this knocks hell out of the poor little eggs and produces something more reminiscent of a cod's roe cream.

from Beryl Reid, Actress

Beryl's summer starter

To serve 4

3 ripe avocado pears	dash of tabasco
2 large cartons cottage cheese	shrimps
juice of 3 lemons	sour cream
1 clove garlic	chives
pepper and salt	

Mix avocado flesh, cottage cheese, lemon juice, crushed garlic, pepper and salt and tabasco well together, add shrimps, pour a little sour cream over the top, sprinkle with chopped chives. Serve with Melba toast. LOVELY.

from Arthur Boyd, Painter

Green salad

My favourite food is a green salad dressed with oil, garlic, lemon and herbs, and I am prepared to eat this as an hors d'œuvre or at any other time.

from Graham Hill, Racing Driver
Mushroom rolls

½ lb. fresh mushrooms   1 loaf (very fresh) unsliced white
1½ tablesp. butter   bread
½ teasp. white pepper

Wipe mushrooms clean with damp cloth, chop very fine, add pepper and sauté for about 5 minutes in butter. Stir frequently.

Cut crusts from bread and slice as thin as possible. (You may be able to get your baker to do this, but if you cannot, you can roll the slices thinner with a rolling pin.) Spread slices generously with mushrooms, and roll. Cut roll in halves or thirds and place on a baking tray. Place under the grill to heat through and brown.

Rolls can be refrigerated or frozen (defrost before browning) and put under the grill when required. ½ lb. mushrooms makes about 2½ dozen rolls.

from Ken Barrington, Journalist, ex England and Surrey Cricketer
Avocado pear and prawns

To serve 2

1 avocado pear   mayonnaise
fresh prawns or a tin of prawns   Worcester sauce
tomato ketchup

Cut the avocado pear in half and remove the stone. Place on a dish and pile the prawns on to the pear. Mix together a quantity of tomato ketchup and mayonnaise, adding a splash of Worcester sauce. Pour over the prawns, and serve.

from Roy Castle, Comedian, Dancer, Musician
Consommé surprise

A delicious dinner party starter or supper dish for four persons.

4 soft-boiled eggs, peeled   peeled, cooked shrimps, prawns
1 tin Crosse and Blackwell   asparagus tips or
   consommé   soured cream for garnish

Place eggs in individual ramekins or soup dishes. Fill each with melted consommé, surround eggs with shrimps, prawns or asparagus tips. Chill in refrigerator. At serving time, garnish top of egg with a spoonful of soured cream.

from Joan Sutherland, Opera Singer

Marinated shrimps

equal quantities of mushrooms
and shrimps; allow about
9–12 shrimps per person,
depending on size

chopped parsley
2 tablesp. lemon juice
4 tablesp. olive oil
freshly ground pepper

Combine all and after tossing several times let marinate for about 1 hour. Serve on lettuce leaf with parsley.

SOUPS

from Rachel Kempson, Actress

Cold avocado soup

To serve 2

2 small, ripe avocados
¾ pt chicken stock (or chicken
bouillon cube)
juice of 1 lemon, or to taste

Peel and slice avocados and blend in electric blender with stock and lemon juice until a creamy consistency is obtained. Pour into individual bowls and put in fridge until cold. The addition of chopped parsley as garnish is attractive.

from Paul Johnson, Author, former Editor of the *New Statesman*

Connemara leek soup

I emphasize that this recipe is not *haute cuisine* or even *cuisine bourgeoise*, but a simple, peasant-type dish – good value for money.

To serve 6

4 medium-sized leeks
1 oz. butter
1 qt stock or water
½ cupful porage oats
salt and pepper

Wash leeks carefully, chopping off most of the green part, then running the tops, in which you've made cross splits, under fierce cold water. Chop into ½-inch chunks and sweat on very low heat in the melted butter. When they are soft and yellowish, add stock or water, seasoning and porage oats. Stir well, then simmer for about 20 minutes.

from Derek Nimmo, Actor

Artichoke soup

This is my favourite soup, often made and served by my wife at dinner parties.

To serve 6–8

1½ lb. Jerusalem artichokes	1 oz. flour (good weight)
1 large onion	1 egg
2 oz. butter	½ gill cream
1 pt water	salt and white pepper
1 pt milk, and ½ gill extra	

Peel artichokes and set aside. Slice onion and soften in the butter without allowing it to colour. Add the artichokes, sliced; cover the pan and shake over fairly low heat for 7–8 minutes. Remove from heat, add water, season, bring to the boil and simmer for 15–20 minutes.

Now put through a nylon sieve or fine Mouli and return to the pan. Blend the flour with ½ gill of cold milk, strain into the pan and stir until boiling. Simmer for a few minutes, then beat the egg, add the cream and add this to the soup as for a liaison. Serve with croûtons of bread.

(Ed: If peeled artichokes are put into a bowl of water with a few drops of lemon juice until required, they will not discolour.)

from Norman Shrapnel, Journalist and Critic

Iced consommé

To serve 4

¼ lb. cream cheese
1 carton yoghourt

1 small tin consommé
garlic

Mix the cheese and yoghourt with half the tin of consommé. Beat well, season, and add a small quantity of finely chopped garlic to taste. Put into small dishes and pour the rest of the consommé on top of the mixture. Leave in the refrigerator for several hours before serving.

from Malcolm Muggeridge, Author, Journalist, Television Personality

Lentil soup

To serve 4

4 oz. lentils
3 pts water
2 chicken bouillon cubes

1 medium-sized onion
1 carrot. diced
salt and pepper

Cook the lentils gently in the water with bouillon cubes added and salt and pepper to taste, for half an hour. Add carrot, diced, and onion cut up, and simmer until tender. Rub through a sieve and serve with chopped parsley.

from Lulu, Singer
Cucumber soup

Here is a favourite soup recipe of mine. Not only is it delicious to eat but it is quick and easy to make.

To serve 4

2 cucumbers
1 onion, chopped
1 pt chicken stock (or use 2 chicken bouillon cubes)
1 pt water
¼ pt single cream
parsley

First cut up the two cucumbers without peeling. Keep a little back for garnish and simmer the rest with the chopped onion in a pint of water until tender. Then sieve. Add 1 pt of chicken stock to this purée and simmer again about 10 minutes. Just before serving, stir ¼ pt single cream into the soup, and decorate the top with chopped parsley and shredded cucumber.

from Jonathan Burn, Actor
Cream of onion soup

Too many cooks who know their onions have been spoiled by this broth. I can thoroughly recommend it.

To serve 4

¾ lb onions	1 pt water
2 oz butter or margarine	salt and pepper
1½ level tablesp. flour	½ pt milk

Peel and slice the onions fairly thinly. Melt the butter or margarine in a saucepan, put in the onion rings and cook gently over low heat stirring often until they are rather tender and a pale golden colour – about 10 mins. Sprinkle in the flour, and stir again until it is absorbed by the fat. Add the water slowly, stirring constantly, add salt and pepper and bring the soup slowly to boiling point. Reduce heat, cover the pan and allow to simmer for 10–15 minutes or until onions are quite soft. Now add the milk, stir again, reheat until almost but not quite boiling, correct the seasoning, and serve very hot. You can, if you like, put this soup through a sieve and if you want a richer soup, add a little cream. But it's very good as it is, with pieces of recognizable onion floating in it.

from Ken Russell, Film Director
Tchaikovsky bortsch

This recipe was adapted from a more elaborate one to celebrate the start of filming *Tchaikovsky*. It's surprisingly easy and good.

To serve 4–6

2 large onions	salt
3 raw beetroots	black pepper
4–5 large tomatoes	a little dill if possible; failing
4 oz. butter	that, fennel or even parsley
1½ pts beef stock (or 2 beef cubes	will do
in 1½ pts water)	large pot of sour cream
1 lemon	

Finely chop onions and soften in the butter in a large saucepan. Shred beetroots finely and add to onions. Roughly chop tomatoes and add those too. Pour on beef stock, bring to the boil and simmer for about 30 minutes, adding the juice of the lemon, salt and black pepper.

Cooked beetroot can be used but should not be added until the last ten minutes of cooking time or the lovely red colour will be lost. Both raw and cooked beets are grated in a few seconds on a cheese grater.

The soup, sprinkled with chopped dill, fennel or parsley, should be served in deep soup plates with a large dollop of sour cream in the centre of each, and a chaser of ice-cold vodka at the side.

from Donald Swann, Composer

Peasant bortsch

There are as many recipes for bortsch as there are transliterations of the Russian letter Щ and they vary from a complex and sophisticated dish to a simple peasant beetroot soup. I have learnt from tasting experience that the bortsch we have here at home which comes from my mother's recipe (she was Russian) is nearer the peasant soup than the more elaborate bortsch you would get in a London restaurant.

To serve 4

1 large onion	1 large cabbage
2 carrots	2 large raw beetroots
2 or 3 rashers streaky bacon	stock or water
a little dripping or other fat	salt and pepper

Chop bacon and all vegetables coarsely. Fry onion, carrot and bacon gently together in a large saucepan in a little dripping or other fat. Add stock and the peeled, chopped, raw beetroot and cabbage. Add more stock to cover vegetables well. Season. Cook until beetroot is tender.

You can strain out some of the vegetables before serving if you like, although this is a thick soup and they are meant to be eaten. This bortsch is good reheated.

from Sheila Black, Woman's Editor, the *Financial Times*

Lemon and orange soup

To serve 4

4 lemons
4 oranges
about 3 dessertsp. demerara or
   soft brown sugar
4 large onions

about 2 pts good chicken or meat
   stock
salt and pepper
fresh double cream
chopped parsley

Squeeze the fruit and leave the juice to stand with brown sugar to taste. (I suggest you experiment on this as people's sweet tastes vary so. The juice should not be sweetened enough to taste 'sweet' but just so that it has some acidity without making your face screw up when you taste it.) Now cover the onions with good meat stock in a deepish pan. Chicken stock is best but any good meat should do. Add the skins of the oranges and lemons on top of the onions, cover the pan and bring to the boil. Simmer for about 15 minutes. Remove lemon and orange skins and purée the remaining mixture, then add the fruit juices and season with salt and pepper to taste.

Either re-warm or chill the soup according to whether you plan to serve it hot or cold. Just before serving, stir in chopped parsley and fresh double cream. The mixture, without cream and parsley, can be kept, sealed, in a fridge for some days.

Lemon and orange soup is highly adaptable. For those who don't have to worry about their figures, a mixture of potato and onion in the basic stock makes a better soup base than merely the onion. For those who have to watch their weight, however, try making a purée of raw cucumber, adding very little stock to it before adding the fruit juices, because cucumber makes so much liquid. Then cheat, and add the cream and parsley. Excellent, whether you're fat or thin.

All variations eat well either hot or cold. I'm not the type who decorates dishes, but you could shave off enough peel to decorate each bowl with a twist of orange and lemon on the rim.

from Rayner Heppenstall, Novelist and Critic

Chicken soup for two

No more than two plates of good stock can be extracted from the carcase of one roast chicken. Strained off the bones, it must be left overnight and thoroughly skimmed next day. Then something a bit fancy must be done with it. Greek lemon soup (which, I understand, may equally be made with beef stock) is too acid for my taste, and I don't care for rice thickening. Dispense with rice, and use far less lemon juice, that of not more than a quarter of a lemon for the stock from one chicken carcase.

the stock made from one chicken carcase

yolk of one egg

juice of a quarter of a lemon

salt

Heat the strained and skimmed stock. Mix a little of it with the yolk of one egg. Stir this mixture into the rest of the stock. Add the lemon juice (and what salt you want). Heat again, very gently, so that the soup just begins to thicken. If you get it too hot, the egg will scramble. Serve with freshly fried croûtons.

from Edward Hyams, Novelist, Journalist, Pamphleteer, Authority on Great Gardens

Lazy soup

I am no cook and frequently a reluctant eater, but I can live on soup.

To serve 2

1 tin of Heinz tomato soup	some single cream
1 small tin of Spanish sweet peppers	parsley, finely chopped
	garlic if liked

Open the tin of soup, empty into a saucepan, add cream to your taste and heat very gently. Do not boil. Meanwhile, open tin of sweet peppers, cut them into small pieces and place in soup bowls. Pour on the soup. Sprinkle with parsley, finely chopped, and a fine sprinkle of chopped garlic if liked. Allow to cool. Place in the refrigerator and serve very chilled. The addition of the peppers takes away the over-sweetness of the tomato soup.

from Katie Stewart, Cookery Journalist

Soupe aux moules

Mussels make a delicious soup and this recipe with wine and cream added has a delicate flavour and an attractive, creamy white appearance. Care should be taken to thoroughly clean the mussels before starting the recipe. No sand or grit should remain on the shells.

To serve 4

1 qt mussels	2 oz. flour
1 pt water	2 oz. butter
1 small onion, finely chopped	2–3 tablesp. single cream
½ pt dry white wine	2 tablesp. coarsely chopped parsley
salt and freshly milled pepper	

Scrub and clean the mussels in several changes of cold water. Remove the beards and discard any mussels that remain open or ones with broken shells. Place in a large saucepan with the water. Cover, and place over a high heat. Cook for 2–3 minutes or until the mussels have opened. Strain and reserve the cooking liquor. Discard any mussels that have not opened, then remove the open shells from most of the mussels – leave a few for decoration. Set mussels aside.

Place the onion in a saucepan and add the white wine. Bring to the boil and simmer gently for about 5 minutes to cook the onion. Add the mussel liquor and season to taste with salt and freshly milled pepper. On a flat plate, blend the butter and flour together to make a *beurre manié*. Then add the mixture in pieces to the hot liquid. Stir to blend the mixture, then bring to the boil stirring until thickened. Stir in the cream and chopped parsley and add the reserved mussels. Heat through for a few moments but do not allow to boil. Serve in a shallow soup plate.

Editor's Note: The recipes in this Section tend to be somewhat repetitive. There are obvious firm favourites such as various versions of what started out in life as Quiche Lorraine; and similar ways of cooking spaghetti. However, I make no apology for including them as they stand, as they mostly have small, interesting touches which put the stamp of the contributor on them or lift them out of the rut.

from The Rev. The Lord Soper, Methodist Minister

Eggs with cheese sauce

To serve 2

3 eggs, hard boiled
white cheese sauce

Cheddar cheese

Slice the eggs and place at the bottom of a shallow dish. Cover with cheese sauce and top with grated Cheddar cheese. Place under a grill and brown. Serve with hot buttered rolls and grilled tomatoes.

from Edward de Bono, Thinker
Eggs de Bono

As far as I know the following recipe is original. The point is to get away from the idea that when one is cooking a particular food it should all be cooked for the same length of time or even the same way. This particular recipe combines some of the huge variety of textures that can be obtained from eggs.

To serve 2

5 eggs	black pepper
butter	two slices of toast

Boil 2 eggs for over 10 minutes, let them stand for a while in cold water, then shell them. Remove the hard-boiled yolks from the whites.

Lightly beat 3 other eggs in a dish. Put some butter into a pan and when it is melted add the hard-boiled whites which have been cut into thin strips or small pieces. Over a low heat stir for a short while, then add the beaten eggs and continue as for scrambled eggs. Serve on buttered toast.

Take the hard-boiled yolks (half at a time) and using the back of a spoon force the yolks through a sieve or strainer so that a fine yellow moss of yolk is deposited on top of the cooked eggs. Continue until all the yolk has been used up in this way. (It may be necessary to scrape the yolk from the outside of the sieve.) Put lots of freshly ground black pepper on top.

from Eric Porter, Actor

Swiss eggs

I love eggs in any form, except possibly thrown at me during a performance: poached, boiled, fried, scrambled, en cocotte – you name it, I've eaten it. But one of my favourite quick egg dishes, which is just right for after a show, very filling but not too heavy and reasonably economical, is Swiss eggs. The Swiss bit comes from the cheese, which should be Gruyère, but I suppose if you use Cheddar, you can call it Oeufs aux Caves!

To serve 2

2–3 oz. Gruyère cheese (thinly
   sliced)
salt and pepper
nutmeg

4 eggs
2 tablesp. double cream
a little butter

Butter a shallow, fireproof dish. Line with thin slices of cheese and season liberally with salt, pepper and nutmeg. Break in eggs and touch yolks gently so that they spread evenly with whites. Season as before. Spoon cream on top, cover with more cheese, season again as before and dot with small pieces of butter. Cook in the centre of a moderate oven 375°F. Mark 5 for approximately 30 minutes. Accompanied by a tossed green salad, the result is delicious.

from The Earl of Lichfield, Photographer
Eggs in pastry cases

To serve 6

6 small pastry cases	seasoning
6 eggs	a little milk
butter	1 teasp. brandy
flour	a dash of Worcester sauce
2 tablesp. tomato purée	¼ lb. fresh shrimps

Poach 6 eggs or make *oeufs mollets*. Leave to stand in cold water so whites do not harden. Make a roux and add two tablespoons of tomato purée, seasoning and a little milk, so consistency is creamy. Then add brandy, a dash of Worcester sauce and ½ lb. fresh shrimps.

Place eggs in hot water for 10 minutes and heat pastry cases in oven. Put eggs in pastry cases and cover with sauce. Serve immediately.

from Keith Michell, Actor and Singer
Tortilla Español

To serve 3–4

5 large potatoes	a few green peas or a green
3 large Spanish onions	pepper
5–6 large eggs	oil (preferably olive)
salt and pepper	

Dice the potatoes and fry in hot oil until golden and *crisp*. At the same time, slice the onions and fry also until golden and *crisp*. While waiting for these to cook, beat the eggs. Then mix potato and onion together in one large pan, pour over the egg mixture, add salt and pepper to taste and a few green peas or some chopped green pepper for colour. Allow to cook without disturbing and when it looks firm, turn omelette out on to a large platter (the Spanish have a special earthenware platter with a handle underneath which will stand on the table) and then slide it carefully back into pan to cook the other side. When ready the tortilla should be turned back on to the platter and served straight away. A green salad is a good accompaniment.

from James Mason, Actor
A way of doing spaghetti

A lot of people in England make do with the soft mush that comes in cans. Even in Italian restaurants spaghetti is usually over-cooked, having been prepared *en masse*. It is important that the teeth bite on to something firm. So . . .

spaghetti	anchovies
olive oil	parsley
shallots	grated Parmesan cheese

Put some fine olive oil in a frying pan. Add chopped shallots and heat until golden. Remove from heat and add chopped anchovies. Cook the spaghetti for about 7 minutes.* Strain, and place in heated bowl. Pour on the sauce and add chopped parsley. Mix and serve with freshly grated Parmesan.

  * This would have to be a very thin spaghetti. *Ed.*

from Colin Cowdrey, Kent and England Cricketer
Spaghetti bolognese

To serve 4

1½ oz. dripping	½ pt stock
1 large onion	2 tablesp. concentrated tomato
1 lb. fine minced beef steak	purée
flour	bouquet garni

salt and pepper
¾ lb. spaghetti
1 oz. butter

grated cheese
water cress

Melt dripping in a large frying pan, add finely chopped onion and sauté until light brown in colour. Sprinkle flour on the minced steak and add to the onion. Cook over fairly strong heat for a few minutes, stirring all the time. Pour on stock, season and bring to the boil. Add purée and bouquet garni; season and simmer for 40–45 minutes, stirring regularly.

Boil the spaghetti in a large saucepan, stirring occasionally to prevent sticking, for approximately 20 minutes;* drain, return to pan and melt butter with it. Turn into hot dish. Remove bouquet garni from sauce and pour over spaghetti. Garnish with water cress and serve, piping hot, with the grated cheese.

* 12–15 minutes is more usual. *Ed.*

from Tom Stoppard, Playwright

Spaghetti Rubery, Worc.

For years I was puzzled by the fact that Italian restaurants from Soho to Umbria, from the trendiest trat to the crummiest coffee bar, were incapable of making a decent sauce to go on the Spaghetti Bolognese while my wife, born near Birmingham, got it right every time. In the end I discovered that all those Italian chefs were actually producing the genuine article and that I didn't like Bolognese sauce, it being about as boring as a wimpy beaten to death in tomato purée. What I liked was sauce Rubery, Worc. It's something to do with the sugar she puts in, I think.

To serve 2

6 oz. spaghetti
2 oz. onion
1 clove garlic
oil
8 oz. fresh minced beef
1 level tablesp. tomato purée

salt, pepper, sugar (to taste)
4 leaves basil or ½ teasp. dried basil
1 8 oz. can peeled tomatoes
a little water if necessary
Parmesan cheese

Finely chop the onion. Crush the garlic. Fry together in oil until golden. Add the minced beef, stir and cook for several minutes. Stir in the tomato purée, salt, pepper and sugar (to taste), and the basil, and finally the canned tomatoes and their juice. Cover the pan and simmer very gently for at least 30 minutes (longer is better), stirring from time to time and adding a little water if the sauce gets too thick.

Cook the spaghetti. Remove sauce from heat, add 2 oz. grated Parmesan cheese, pour over spaghetti and serve with extra cheese sprinkled on top.

from Thora Hird, Actress
Spaghetti savoury

I recommend this tasty recipe. Pop it into the oven whilst watching television, then serve on a tray with a glass of red wine and relax.

To serve 1

3 oz. long spaghetti	a pinch of mixed herbs
½ lb. onions	1 can (14 oz.) peeled tomatoes
2 oz. butter	6 oz. strong Cheddar cheese
salt and pepper	

Peel and slice onions, fry in the butter until tender and pale golden brown. Place in ovenproof dish and season with salt, pepper and herbs.

Break dry spaghetti into 3-inch lengths and scatter over top of onion, then pour can of tomatoes over to cover spaghetti. Grate cheese in an even layer over the top. Cover with kitchen foil or lid and bake in a slow oven 310°F. Mark 2 for 1¾ hours.

Remove foil, raise heat to 375°F. Mark 5 for 10–15 minutes to brown. Serve at once.

from Lyndon Brook, Actor and Writer
Pasticcio of macaroni

Ideal for supper after the theatre. A green salad goes very well
with it, and of course a glass of wine.

To serve 6–8

3 large onions, diced
½ glass water
1 teasp. cinnamon
2 lb. ground steak
1 small can tomatoes
salt and black pepper
½ teasp. ground nutmeg

½ lb. macaroni
1½ tablesp. butter
1 teasp. cornflour
6 eggs
1 pt milk
5–6 oz. Parmesan cheese

Simmer the onions in a thick-bottomed pan with 1 teasp. salt
and the cinnamon and water for ½ hour. Add the ground steak
and stir until all water is absorbed and the meat is browned.
Add the tomatoes, nutmeg and black pepper to taste. Cook
until liquid from tomatoes is nearly absorbed. Meanwhile, cook
the macaroni, strain, and add to meat mixture, stirring well.
Beat 3 eggs and add together with ¼ lb. grated Parmesan. Put in
well-greased deep baking-dish and pour 1 tablesp. melted butter
over top of mixture.

Now melt ½ tablesp. butter in a pan, add the cornflour slaked
in a bare pint of milk. Beat the other 3 eggs and add, stirring
until creamy. Pour this over the mixture in the baking-dish and
sprinkle Parmesan over the top. Bake half an hour in moderate
oven 350°F. Mark 4.

from The Rt Hon. Judith Hart, M.P.
Macaroni mix-up

To serve up to 6

3 largish onions
1 clove garlic (can be left out, of
course)

oil
1 pckt of Quick Quaker macaroni
1 green pepper

1 red pepper (if you have it)	1 level dessertsp. paprika
4 rashers lean bacon	oregano
3 tomatoes	salt
¼ lb. mushrooms (if you like them)	freshly ground pepper
	grated Parmesan cheese

In a heavy pot, melt the onions, chopped, and the garlic, crushed, in 3–4 tablesp. oil. Add thinly sliced peppers and the bacon, roughly chopped. Cook gently for about 10 minutes (until everything is cooked but still retaining separate identity). Then add the tomatoes, skinned and chopped, and salt, pepper, paprika and a good sprinkling of oregano. Cook for a further few minutes.

In the meantime, cook plenty of macaroni in another pan. Drain well. Mix everything together. Serve with grated Parmesan cheese and warm French bread.

The addition of mushrooms is very optional. If you use them, add them roughly chopped with the tomatoes. I suppose that one could use rice instead of macaroni, and turn it into a risotto. But I never have.

from Johnny Morris, Entertainer
Bacon and laver

A meal for meditation. Laver is a seaweed specially prepared and sold here and there, generally at a fishmongers. It has a subtle flavour.

¼ lb. bacon	½ lb. laver or laverbread

Fry the bacon, remove from pan and keep warm. Fry or warm through the laver or laverbread in the bacon fat. Serve on warm plate and sprinkle with pepper. Eat in complete silence. You should have some exceptional thoughts generate in your head when you are about half-way through.

from Margaret Drabble, Author
Butter beans and bacon

Very cheap recipe for delicious supper, stolen from a friend.
Obvious advantages: extreme simplicity and low cost.

To serve 3–4

½ lb. bacon
1½ lb. tomatoes
1–2 onions

garlic, herbs, etc., optional
2 tins butter beans

Chop everything up (except beans). Fry bacon gently, add
onions when the bacon fat runs, garlic if used, then tomatoes
and seasonings. Cook until soft. Add beans. Heat. Eat.

from The Rt Hon. John Davies, M.P., Secretary for Trade
and Industry and President of the Board of Trade
Jambon au béchamel

hearts of celery or endive
  (chicory) parboiled
an equal number of thin slices of
  lean cooked ham
béchamel sauce
grated cheese

For the béchamel:
4 oz. butter or margarine
2 heaped tablesp. plain flour
pepper and salt
½ pt milk

Wrap the celery hearts or endives in the slices of ham and place
in rows in an ovenware dish, preferably large and shallow.

Cover with béchamel sauce, sprinkle liberally with grated cheese and cook in moderate oven 380°F. Mark 5, on highest shelf for about 20 minutes or until brown.

To make the béchamel, melt the butter or margarine, add the flour with pepper and only a pinch of salt, and cook whilst stirring continuously. When a paste is formed, add slowly, always stirring, ½ pt milk, and cook until sauce is as thick or as liquid as you like it.

from Tony Cawley, Comedian

Ham cornets with cheese and pineapple

To serve 4

1½ lb. peeled new potatoes
¼ pt mayonnaise
a few chives
8 slices ham
4 oz. cream cheese

16 oz. can pineapple rings
  drained
salt and pepper
cress for garnish

Cook potatoes in salted water until just tender, drain and dice. Snip chives into mayonnaise and mix well. Toss potatoes in this while they are still warm. Chill.

Chop two pineapple rings small. Roll ham slices into cone shapes and fill with a mixture of cream cheese and chopped pineapple. Season to taste with salt and pepper. Chill.

Pile potato salad in the centre of a plate, arrange stuffed cornets around the edge. Garnish with cress behind each cornet and a quarter of a pineapple ring on top. Make a cut in the last pineapple ring, twist and place on top of potato salad.

from Nigel Calder, Science Writer

Quiche Lorraine

You can meet bacon, egg and cheese flan anywhere: hot with salad and wine to start a grand dinner, lukewarm (usually) at a party, or cold for a picnic lunch. It's always tasty and nourishing. But it was at l'Orangerie in San Francisco (on O'Farrell) that the Quiche Lorraine brought home to me how a French chef can turn the commonest ingredients into gastronomic poetry.

short crust pastry
bacon
2 eggs
½ lb. assorted cheeses (grated)

anything else you fancy, cream,
    mushrooms, capers
pepper

Line a flan tin with short crust pastry. Lightly fry some bacon, chop it and scatter it on the pastry. Beat up a couple of eggs with half a pound of assorted cheeses (grated) and add anything else you fancy – cream, mushrooms, capers – not forgetting plenty of pepper. Pour the mixture into the flan and bake till brown in a moderate oven.

from Dora Bryan, Actress
Cheese and onion pie

6 oz. short crust pastry
2 Spanish onions, chopped
4 oz. cheese, diced
2 rashers bacon, chopped

2 eggs
¼ pt cream
salt and pepper

Line flan tin with pastry and bake blind for about ¼ hour. Fry onions gently in a little butter till golden brown. Fry bacon gently in same fat. Beat eggs with cream till slightly thick. Arrange onions, cheese and bacon in pastry case, pour well-seasoned cream and egg mixture over and return to oven for about 30 minutes at 375°F. Mark 5.

from Richard Rodney Bennett, Composer
Jean's egg and bacon pie

½ lb. bacon, or ham or garlic
    sausage

1 large onion
¼ pt milk

black pepper

1 cardamom seed

½ lb. short crust pastry (or 1 frozen packet)

2 eggs

large handful grated Cheddar cheese (Black Diamond is best)

Set oven at 425°F. Mark 7 (hot). Chop bacon and onion, gently simmer in milk with cardamom and pepper (because of the bacon you won't need salt). Beat eggs separately. When bacon is tender, strain off milk and save, remove cardamom seed and allow bacon and onion to cool. Line shallow pie dish or flan tin with pastry, put in bacon and onion mixture; mix eggs with as much of the milk as will fill the dish (with a bit of space to spare for rising) and pour over. Sprinkle cheese on top. Bake for about 20–25 minutes, watching that cheese doesn't burn.

from Jane Asher, Actress

Savoury pie

½ lb. short crust pastry

2 large onions

½ lb. sharp cheese, grated

¼ lb. ripe tomatoes

1 clove garlic

small pinch mixed herbs

2 oz. butter

1 egg

salt, black pepper

Line a greased 8-inch pie plate with the pastry. Put it in the fridge while you peel and slice the onions and fry them in the butter until golden. Slice the tomatoes and chop the garlic very finely. Put a layer of onions on the pastry-lined pie plate, add salt and pepper, then a layer of tomatoes sprinkled with the chopped garlic and the herbs and finally a layer of cheese. Repeat the layers and top with pastry. Make three cuts in the top crust to let out the steam, seal the edges, brush with beaten egg and bake in a pre-heated moderate oven for 45 minutes until golden brown. Serve hot.

This is a cheap and fairly quick delicious supper dish which can, of course, be made without the tomatoes and herbs as a simple cheese and onion pie.

from Trevor Nunn, Artistic Director of the Royal Shakespeare Company

Quiche aux fruits de mer

uncooked pastry shell	3 eggs
2 tablesp. chopped shallots	¼ pt cream
1½ oz. butter	1 tablesp. tomato purée
4 oz. butter	1 oz. grated cheese
4 oz. shellfish	salt and pepper
2 tablesp. port or madeira	

Cook the shallots in the butter for one or two minutes over a moderate heat until tender but not browned. Add the shellfish, and stir gently for two minutes. Season. Add the wine, raise the heat and boil for a moment. Allow to cool slightly.

Beat the eggs in a mixing bowl with the cream, tomato purée and seasonings. Gradually blend in the shellfish mixture. Pour this filling into the pastry shell and sprinkle with the cheese. Bake in a moderate oven for 25–30 minutes until the quiche has puffed and browned.

from Alun Owen, Playwright

Quiche à l'oignon

6 oz. puff or short crust pastry	2 tablesp. cream
1 lb. onions	2 oz. grated cheese
2 oz. butter or bacon fat	salt and black pepper
2 eggs	

Fry the sliced onions gently in the butter until tender and pale gold. Line a deep 7-inch flan ring with the pastry, making sure it is well pressed down in the tin. Beat eggs, add cream, grated cheese, and seasoning. Add to onions. Pour this mixture into the pastry case carefully.

If puff pastry: bake for 15 minutes in the centre of a very hot oven (425°F. Mark 7) then lower heat for a further 30 minutes. If short crust pastry: bake for 15 minutes in hot oven (400°F. Mark 6) then lower to moderate for a further 30 minutes.

from Honor Wyatt, Journalist and Broadcaster

Cod's roe pie

To serve 6

2 lb. fresh cod's roe	1 ½ tablesp. corn oil
chopped parsley	1 teasp. lemon juice
1 breakfast cup breadcrumbs	mashed potato
3 hard-boiled eggs	butter
1 teasp. anchovy paste	salt and pepper

Boil roe about 15 minutes. Skin, and chop in small pieces. Mix with chopped parsley, chopped eggs, breadcrumbs, anchovy paste, oil, lemon juice, salt and pepper. Put in dish, cover with mashed potato, dot with butter. Can be put aside and, when required, baked in medium oven for about ½ hour.

from Eirlys Roberts, Journalist, Head of Research and Editorial Division of the Consumers' Association

Paella (very British version)

To serve 6

12 tablesp. *long grain* rice	olive oil
2 lb. onions	2 lb. tomatoes

salt and pepper
1 small tin chicken
1 tin tunny
1 tin prawns
2 oz. nuts

2 oz. raisins
1 tin pineapple
¼ lb. mushrooms
½ tin anchovies

Add the rice gradually to a large pan full of boiling, slightly salted water. Allow to boil for 12½ minutes precisely. Drain rice, dry and keep warm. Meanwhile fry the onions in the olive oil till golden brown. Add the tomatoes, cool and season. Then add everything else. When piping hot all through, add to rice and serve.

from Kaye Webb, Journalist, Editor of Puffin Books

Elvira's paella

When I want a party dish which can be kept waiting and served as a buffet supper, I use the recipe which was first made for us (and happily still is) by a delightful Spanish lady called Elvira. This is enough for six – for more people double up the quantities accordingly.

To serve 6

1 chicken, boned and cut up into small, bite-sized pieces
1 onion
5–6 tomatoes
1–2 pimentos
not less than 4 oz. shelled shrimps, prawns, flaked fish (tuna) or scallops, or any combination of these
2 large cups rice

1 clove garlic
salt
pinch of saffron
a little water
oil left from pan ⎫ mix thoroughly with pestle and mortar
6 cups water
1 small pkt frozen peas or green beans for colour
oil (about 2 tablesp.)

Heat some good quality oil in a pan – about 2 tablespoons – put in pieces of chicken and brown on both sides for about 12 minutes. Transfer into a casserole. Then fry tomatoes, pimentos and onions in remaining oil. Cook sliced scallops if using them, otherwise put vegetables and fish into casserole with a little water (¼ cup) and cook with the lid on for about 15–20 minutes.

While this is cooking, mix the saffron, garlic, salt and any oil left from the pan with a pestle and mortar.

After 20 minutes stir saffron and garlic into the casserole, add rice and 6 cups of water, and cook *uncovered* for 25 minutes, adding more water if necessary. When the chicken is tender, add peas and beans.

When it has finished cooking, put on the lid and leave in the oven on a very low light to keep warm until needed.

from Michael Ayrton, Painter, Sculptor, Author, and Elisabeth Ayrton, novelist and writer of cookery books

Painters' toasted cheese

My husband no longer cooks because he (rightly!) maintains that it would be absurd to do so when married to me. This, however, is a recipe from his unmarried past which I frequently make for snack lunch or late supper. It is always known in our household and in others which have adopted it as Painters' Toasted Cheese.

For each person

2 oz. Cheddar cheese   1 dessertsp. milk
1 oz. butter   1 round of toast
salt and plenty of black pepper

Cut the cheese up into roughly ¼ inch cubes and stir in a bowl with the slightly softened butter and the milk and seasoning. Work them together with a wooden spoon, so that you have a sort of paste (which need not be smooth). Pile this on the lightly toasted bread and spread to cover all corners. Toast under medium hot grill until smooth, creamy and golden brown.

The consistency is different from both ordinary toasted cheese and from Welsh Rarebit. The hungry painter, when flush, placed two grilled rashers of bacon on top and a grilled tomato cut in half and two grilled mushrooms on top of the rashers, but poorer painters had to be content with the cheese alone.

from Vilem Tausky, Musician
Brains from Brno

This is a luncheon or supper dish which was often served by my Viennese mother but is equally well prepared by my English wife. It is satisfying but easily digested and makes an excellent after-theatre dish.

2 sets of brains	2 oz. butter
1 medium cauliflower	salt and pepper
4 large eggs	dried breadcrumbs for topping

Cut away all stalk from the cauliflower, divide into flowerets and boil in salted water until tender but not mashy. Meanwhile, blanch the brains in boiling water for at least 5 minutes, then remove the membranes and cut into walnut-sized pieces.

Melt the butter in a frying pan and cook the brains in it very gently for about 5 minutes. Mix the cauliflower and brains lightly together. Well beat the eggs, season to taste and pour over the mixture in the frying pan. It will amalgamate in about a minute. Turn the whole mixture into a well buttered, fireproof dish, scatter with breadcrumbs, dot with butter and brown under a hot grill.

from Joan Lestor, M.P.
Savoury bananas

To serve 4

8 bananas	½ pt milk
8 slices ham	4 oz. cheese
2 oz. butter	2 oz. butter
grated cheese	salt and pepper
cheese sauce made from:	

Gently fry bananas in the butter until golden brown. Roll each banana when cooked in a slice of ham and place side by side but not touching in a fireproof dish. Cover with cheese sauce, sprinkle with grated cheese and brown under grill for a few minutes. Serve with a green vegetable.

from Frankie Howerd, Comedian
Veal and ham pie

½ lb. short or flaky pastry
1½ lb. veal (any cut, bones to be reserved for stock)
6 oz. sliced ham (or bacon can be used)
1 egg, hard boiled
1 tablesp. flour
1 teasp. grated lemon rind
a little chopped parsley

salt and pepper
For Stock:
a few veal bones, chopped into fairly small pieces
1 carrot
1 onion
1 stick celery
bouquet garni

Make about 1½ pts stock, skimming off impurities as it comes to the boil, and simmering gently for about 2 hours (or make in pressure cooker).

Cut veal into pieces about 2-inches square, roll in flour seasoned with salt, pepper, chopped parsley and grated lemon rind, and lay in pie dish, alternately with pieces of ham and with a layer of sliced, hard-boiled egg in the middle. Pour in veal stock to come about ¾ way up the dish. Cover with pastry in the usual way, decorating the top with pastry leaves. Make a hole in the centre with a pointed knife or skewer to allow escape of steam. Glaze with milk or white of egg and bake about 2 hours in very hot oven if flaky pastry used and in hot oven if short pastry used, for the first 10 minutes; and then reducing heat to 375°F. Mark 4 for the rest of the time. If pastry browns before meat is cooked, as it probably will, cover with a piece of foil.

Meanwhile, reduce remaining stock by boiling hard. If you doubt its jelling capacity, add a little gelatine. Correct seasoning and when the pie is cooked, pour stock through the hole in the crust, using a funnel, until the pie is filled.

Leave until quite cold and the jelly set firm, but do not put in refrigerator. Refrigeration often toughens pastry.

from Eamonn Andrews, Television Personality
Stuffed bacon fritters

The kind of recipes I like best are those that cater for the Sunday night left-overs. So I pass along a variation of one I picked up some time ago that produces quite a delicious snack without being back-breaking in its demands. It's intended to use whatever the joint is that is left over, when it gets too small to carve without cutting off your thumb in the process.

remains of any joint	batter made with:
3–4 rashers bacon	4 oz. flour
salt, pepper, celery salt, or seasonings to taste	1 egg
	¼ pt water (approx.)
oil for frying	salt

Mince it up finely whatever it is, flavour it with gay abandon, salt, pepper, celery salt – you name it, you put it in if your taste buds fancy it. Remove the rinds from the bacon rashers, cut in half, beat them out as thin as they will stand, and then put the minced meat inside, roll them up and tie them with thread. Meanwhile, prepare a batter – flour, egg, water, salt. Let it stand for a little while, dust the bacon rolls in flour, dip them in the batter and pop them into hot oil until they are a nice crispy golden brown. Delicious.

from Baroness Stocks, Writer, Educationalist, Broadcaster
Bean supper

I have always avoided cooking. Here is my recipe for the nearest
I get to it.

I small tin Heinz baked beans   2 eggs or 2 rashers bacon

Open the tin and tip the contents into a baking dish. Hard-boil
the eggs and place them on top of the baked beans. Cook in the
oven until conveniently warm. For a varied diet, two rashers of
bacon can be substituted for the hard-boiled eggs.

FISH

from Renée Short, M.P.

Fish soup

This is a gorgeous, satisfying fish soup – but a main dish and not what is usually understood by a soup. You need a large saucepan for this quantity, and this will give two meals for four people.

To serve 8

2½ lb. white fish – cod, turbot, halibut, plaice and haddock together
¼ lb. shrimps or prawns
2 scallops
1 qt mussels
3 tablesp. olive oil
1 large onion
1 lb. leeks
2 or 3 sticks celery
chopped parsley to taste
2 bay leaves
2–3 anchovies
1 or 2 cloves garlic
1 medium tin tomato purée
1 wineglass dry white wine
salt and pepper

Heat olive oil in saucepan, add finely chopped onion and cook till brown. Add chopped celery and parsley, the bay leaves, anchovies, crushed garlic, tomato purée and wine, season and cook all together for 5 minutes.

Meanwhile, make stock with fish heads and tails. Then cut up fish into pieces 3–4 inches long, cut scallops in half and add all to saucepan taking care not to break the fish pieces. Cook for 10 minutes, then add enough stock and water to cover the fish. Add leeks cut into pieces and bring all to the boil. Add the cleaned mussels and prawns or shrimps. Cook for another 10 minutes. The mussels should all now be open. Serve at once with sour cream and grated Parmesan or good farmhouse Cheddar cheese. A few black olives can be added with the mussels if liked.

from Roy Boulting, Film Director

Haddock baked in wine

To serve 4

3 lb. fresh haddock (preferably a whole fish)
8 small mushrooms finely chopped
1 small onion finely chopped

2 tablesp. butter
salt and fresh ground pepper
¼ pt dry white wine
2 tablesp. finely chopped parsley

Sauté onion and mushrooms in butter until onion is transparent but not browned. Put skinned and cleaned fish into shallow, buttered baking dish, on a layer of onion and mushrooms. Cover fish with remaining onion and mushrooms, season with salt and pepper and pour all the dry white wine over it. Bake in oven at 380°F. Mark 5 until fish flakes easily with fork. Sprinkle with chopped parsley and serve straight from baking dish.

from Michael Denison, Actor
Michael Denison's fish dish

To serve 4

1½ lb. filleted haddock or cod   1 medium-sized tin of tomatoes
   (fresh)   grated cheese
1 tin condensed mushroom soup   salt and pepper

Place fish in a well-buttered ovenware dish, add the soup and
tomatoes, season well and cover with grated cheese. Bake for
40 minutes in a pre-heated oven at 380°F. Mark 5. Remove from
oven and brown the top gently under the grill. Serve at once
with mashed potato.

from The Rt Hon. Lord Justice Russell
Haddock mousse

To serve 6–8

1 medium-sized smoked haddock   1 pkt savoury white sauce
milk   mixture
2 hard-boiled eggs (9 mins.)   1 large carton double cream
1 tin jellied consommé

Cook haddock in milk and flake the flesh small. Make up the white sauce with liquid from the haddock, and cool. Chop the eggs, add to the haddock and mix with white sauce and consommé. Season to taste. Now whip the cream, fold into the haddock mixture and put into the fridge. Judgement must be used as to the exact amounts of liquids involved.

This recipe saves the trouble of making béchamel and aspic jelly. It is very good.

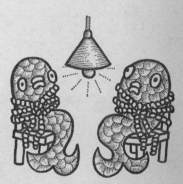

from James Cameron, Journalist, Author, Television Personality

Grilled herrings

I think there is no subject that interests me less than food. I have lived all over the world in countries where cooking is either pedantically good or abysmally awful. In either case the only recipe I nostalgically dwell on is as follows:

Herrings	salt
oatmeal bannocks	butter

Take two fine fat fresh herrings. Grill them, with the roes still in. Eat them, accompanied by oatmeal bannocks, salt and butter.

from Paul Jennings, Author and Journalist
Herrings in oatmeal

All I can make is mashed potatoes. And my favourite recipe
suffers from the fact that someone much more famous than me
has gone on record as saying it's hers too: the Queen Mother in
fact. It's herrings in oatmeal. (Curious relationship between
scarcity and niceness, imagined or otherwise. Should we think
caviare so marvellous if it was as common as herrings, and
vice versa?) Well, my wife says you split and de-backbone
herrings, lay them on a plate of *coarse*, nubbly oatmeal, one
side after the other of course, put them in a frying pan in
which there's some hot fat, turn – and serve with lemon
quarters.

from Richard Murdoch, Stage, Radio and Television Personality
Baked trout with trimmings

1 trout per person	capers
onion	peeled shrimps
mushrooms	butter
salt and black pepper	

Place trout, lightly seasoned with salt and ground black pepper,
in a baking dish with butter. Lightly fry some chopped onions in
butter until golden; first add chopped or sliced mushrooms, then
a few capers and peeled shrimps. Draw a serrated knife across
the top of the trout at intervals roughly ¾ inch apart and baste
with this mixture. Bake in a moderate oven about 15–20 minutes.
Finish by placing baking dish for a few moments under a very
hot grill, to brown. Spoon the other ingredients on top of each
trout when serving.

from Wendy Toye, Film and Stage Director and Choreographer

Marinated kippers

one small packet of filleted kippers	herbs
onion	oil

Skin the kippers and take out any loose bones. Place in dish and cover with thin slices of onion. Sprinkle with herbs and cover in oil. Put a lid on the dish and leave in fridge to marinate for a couple of days. Eat.

from Sir Hugh Casson, Architect

Baked stuffed mackerel

I am not a food lover and take disgracefully little trouble in choosing food, but this dish I always enjoy.

To serve 4

4 mackerel	salt and pepper
¼ lb. mushrooms	a little sweet basil
1 large cooking apple	1 egg
2 slices brown bread	oil
juice and grated rind of 1 lemon	

Split and bone mackerel. Mince apple, mushrooms and bread. Add salt, pepper, basil and juice and rind of lemon. Bind with egg. Insert stuffing in each mackerel and close up. Lay in baking dish, sprinkle with salt, pepper and a little oil. Cover with greased paper and bake slowly for ¾ hour. Serve with salad.

from Eric Thompson, Actor
Moules marinière (1)

If you like shell-fish, this is cheap and delicious.

fresh mussels – say 2 pt per head   lemon juice
  and some over for greed   salt and pepper
cream   wine vinegar

Immerse the mussels in fresh water and scrabble about with the
hands to dislodge sand etc. (if you have just collected them from
the shore you will need to scrabble more but they will certainly
be fresh). Leave for a while and discard any which open or
float about. Then, and this is boring but essential, scrub each
one with a nail brush and put again into fresh water. Drain and
strain. Take a large pan and put the mussels in. Stand on rather
low heat covered with a lid, and cook for 5–10 minutes. Add no
water.

    Tip out into a large container taking care to keep some of the
liquid that will have accumulated. Take some of this liquid – say
about $\frac{3}{4}$ pint. Strain it well through muslin and mingle it lovingly
with some cream, lemon juice, seasoning and a little wine
vinegar until you have a rich, creamy sauce. Eat the mussels
from their shells with the sauce.

from The Reverend Canon L. John Collins
Moules marinière (2)

3 qt mussels   small piece of celery
1 small onion   parsley
1 clove garlic   1 oz. butter
1 small glass white wine $\frac{1}{2}$ oz. flour

Put chopped onion, garlic and celery into a large pan with the
wine and about 1 pt water. Add pepper but not salt. Put in the

well-cleaned mussels, cover the pan and cook until the shells open.

Take out the mussels, keep them hot, and thicken the liquid in which they have cooked with 1 oz. butter and ½ oz. flour. Pour the sauce over the mussels in a large tureen and sprinkle with parsley. Serve very hot.

from Hattie Jacques, Jobbing Actress
Moules matelot

This is the recipe for a first course that is particularly pleasing if none of my guests eat shell-fish because then I can finish the lot.

mussels as required	parsley
garlic	salt and pepper
butter	

Cook in water in the usual manner (about 1 pt water to 3 qts mussels). Remove fish from one half of shell and place in the deeper half. Put a generous portion of garlic butter* on fish. Grill until golden brown. Sprinkle with chopped parsley. Serve.

* (Garlic Butter is made by pounding garlic in a mortar then working butter, a little salt and pepper and plenty of finely chopped parsley into it. *Ed.*)

from Helen Burke, Cookery Writer
Grilled cod steaks

. . . not fillets but slices cut across the bone, preferably from the tail end so that they are compact. But the cuts from further up the body, even with their open ends, are perfectly good. Some people claim that they are even better.

The steaks must be grilled on *one side only*. I wish that I could claim to be the originator of this, but I am not. There was a small very good west-end restaurant where I frequently lunched. During its season, I used to order a grilled salmon steak. I asked the proprietor why it was that his grilled salmon was so moist, so full of flavour and so much better than that served in other restaurants. He could not explain, but one day the solution dawned on me. I turned the steak over and noticed that there was no trace of colour on the under side. Clearly, it had been grilled on one side only. From then onwards, I have always grilled fish cut across the bone – that is, all round fish such as cod, large haddock, hake and, of course, salmon – on one side only and never on the grid.

4 cod steaks, each approx ¾ inch thick	salt, freshly milled pepper
3 oz. butter	flour

Melt 3 oz. butter in the grill pan. Lay the steaks in it, sprinkle them with a little salt and at once turn them so that both sides are coated with the butter. Season them again with salt, and, if iiked, freshly milled pepper and sprinkle them with flour. Place them under a medium hot grill for a few minutes, then increase the heat and baste them with the butter in the pan.

By this time, the juice from the steaks has amalgamated with the butter and the mixture tends to stick to the pan and will soon burn. So this is the moment to spoon 2 to 3 tablesp. of hot water into the pan – not on to the fish – and rotate it (the pan) this way and that to blend the water with the residue in the pan. Baste the fish again and finish the cooking.

When the steaks are a deliciously deep golden tone, they are, probably, cooked through, but test the central bone of one of them with a fork or the finger and thumb. If it moves easily, the steaks are done. If not, give them a little longer: 10–15 minutes in all should be enough, unless the steaks are very thick.

I ought to have said that it is line-caught inshore cod I have in mind – not fish from far-off waters which has been kept on ice on a fishing vessel for possibly several weeks before being landed at one of our home ports. Fish which has had to undergo this long storage has lost much of its fine flavour.

Vegetables: if your grill pan is large enough, half-way through the grilling surround the cod or other fish steaks with mushrooms, gill sides up, and halved tomatoes, cut sides up. Baste the mushrooms with some of the buttery juices in the pan and sprinkle the tomatoes with flour so that they can take on a little colour.

To serve: place the grilled steaks on a heated serving-dish and garnish them with the mushrooms and tomatoes. Add a nice piece of butter, 1 dessertsp. finely chopped parsley and the juice of ½ lemon to the grill pan and barely melt the butter in it. Spoon this sauce over the fish or pass it separately in a sauce boat.

Sweet corn is another vegetable which goes very well with fish. After transferring the grilled fish steaks to a heated serving-dish, sprinkle a little flour into the grill pan and work it into the residue. Place the pan on a not-too-hot hot-plate or a medium-low gas ring. For 4 servings, stir ¼ pt of double cream into the pan and simmer for a few minutes. Add a can of creamed sweet corn and heat through. Taste and add further seasoning, if required.

If preferred, soured cream can be used instead of fresh.

Spinach, either chopped or *en branche* is another good candidate for a fish dish. Wash and drain the spinach, then cook it, covered, in no water other than that which adheres to the wet leaves. Add a little salt.

After adding the flour and cream, as above, turn the drained spinach into the grill pan and heat through.

from Baroness Gaitskell, Politician
Cold sole dish

fillets of sole	vinegar or white wine
court bouillon made from:	onion
water	a few mushrooms

salt and pepper
mayonnaise jelly made from:
1 tablesp. gelatine
1½ cups water

½ cup thick mayonnaise sauce
  (home made)
a few peeled grapes

Make a court bouillon, bring to the boil and reduce well by fast boiling. Poach the fillets of sole in this, about ten minutes, keeping them flat. Lift out on to a flat dish.

Make the mayonnaise jelly: dissolve 1 tablesp. of gelatine in ¼ cup cold water, then add 1¼ cups boiling water. Stir well, and chill slightly. Combine this with the mayonnaise sauce. Chill again. Sprinkle the fillets with a few peeled grapes and cover with the mayonnaise jelly.

from Michael Aspel, Radio and Television Personality
Sole Murat

On a trip to Paris about fifteen years ago, I decided to be courageous — gastronomically — and stuck a pin in the menu. 'Monsieur, that is for specialist palates,' said the waiter, but I insisted. It turned out to be wild pig — black meat, set in a pool of grey sludge. So here's something quite different:

To serve 4–6

4 fillets of sole, cut into strips
½ pt milk
4 oz. seasoned flour
4 oz. butter
8 oz. diced, fried potatoes

12 oz. tin artichoke bottoms,
  diced
2 teasp. lemon juice
1 tablesp. chopped parsley

Dip sole in milk, then in seasoned flour; fry in 2 oz. butter. Add artichoke bottoms and potatoes. Mix together. Brown remaining butter and when it has a nutty smell, add lemon juice. Place fish and vegetables in a serving dish, cover with butter and lemon juice, sprinkle with parsley and serve.

from J. B. Priestley, Novelist, Playwright, Critic
Sole Marrakesh

For each person

2 fillets of Dover sole	butter
1 oz. cooked prawns	salt
1½ oz. Patna rice	flour
a little cooked and chopped	2 egg yolks
lobster	double cream
2 tablesp. white wine	parsley

First make a good fish stock with the sole bones, etc. Be sure to
have enough to poach the fillets and cook the rice. Add the
wine to sufficient stock for the fillets, a nut of butter and a pinch
of salt, and poach the fillets in this gently. Cook the rice in the
rest of the stock and when it is done, stir in the prawns and
lobster to heat thoroughly. Reduce the liquor from the poached
fillets and make a sauce with 1 oz. of butter, 1 dessertsp. plain
flour, 2 egg yolks and 1 tablesp. double cream to each ½ pt
of fish liquor. Season to taste. Arrange the fillets in the centre
of an entrée dish surrounded with the rice and prawns. Pour
the sauce over. Garnish with the chopped parsley.

from Dame Agatha Christie, Author
Lemon sole Greenway

6 fillets of lemon sole	chopped tarragon (or parsley, but
glass of white wine	tarragon is better)
butter	lemon juice
salt and pepper	a teacupful of shrimps
½ pt cream	

Put the fillets of lemon sole in a fireproof dish, add the wine
and a small piece of butter, and put into medium oven until
just beginning to brown.

    Put ½ pt. cream in saucepan and cook, stirring, until it

begins to thicken. Add a tablespoonful or so of chopped tarragon, a little lemon juice and season to taste. Then stir in a teacupful of shrimps, thicken a little more, then pour over the fish and bring to table.

Note: small early carrots, cooked till soft, are very good added to this.

from Michael Bond, Author

Prawn supper dish

This is a good standby from our early married days and has stood the test of time – still giving rise to mouth-watering antici-pation rather than groans of 'not *that* again!' It has the advantage of being reasonably cheap and is ideal for those occasions when the meal may be delayed.

To serve 4

5 hard-boiled eggs	1 tablesp. cornflour
5 good-sized tomatoes	1 oz. butter
3 oz. grated Cheddar cheese	2 oz. peeled prawns
½ pt milk	

Skin the tomatoes by plunging into boiling water for 1 minute. Cut into slices. Also slice the hard-boiled eggs. If frozen prawns are used, allow to thaw out well before using.

Make a cheese sauce by melting the butter, stirring in the cornflour and adding milk, stirring well to prevent the flour turning lumpy. Add the grated cheese and blend well.

Put alternate layers of sliced eggs and tomatoes into a buttered casserole and sprinkle the prawns on evenly. Pour the sauce on top, making sure that the ingredients are all covered. Bake in a fairly hot oven until the top is nicely brown and bubbling. Serve immediately, and if possible with rather small, crisp roast potatoes and green peas.

from Marjorie Proops, Journalist, Radio and Television Personality

Fish in sweet-sour sauce

To serve 4

4 portions of halibut (or 4 good portions of plaice preferably on the bone)	3 lemons
	3 eggs
	castor sugar
4 large onions cut into rings	salt

Cover fish with cold water, add onions, salt as desired, and juice of half a lemon. Poach gently until cooked. Drain fish and onions, saving the stock. Arrange fish on deep dish and place onion rings on top of fish.

Sauce: beat eggs in basin, add juice of remaining $2\frac{1}{2}$ lemons, 1 dessertspoon sugar, pinch salt. Add cooled stock left from fish. The more stock you add, the thinner the sauce will be. Put mixture in saucepan on low heat and stirring all the time, bring nearly to the boil. Boiling will curdle the eggs. Taste for lemony sharpness. If too sharp, stir in a little more sugar.

Pour sauce over fish and onions and allow to cool. Chill before serving and serve with green or chicory salad and garlic bread.*

* To make garlic bread, crush 1 or 2 cloves of garlic with a little salt and work into this about $\frac{1}{4}$ lb. butter. Split a French loaf lengthwise, avoiding cutting right through bottom crust, and fill it with the garlic butter pressing well together again and smearing a little over the outside. Bake in a previously heated oven 425°F. Mark 7 for about 20 minutes or until crisp. *Ed.*

from Lord Reigate, Politician

Fish chowder

This is an old American recipe and was much used on the clippers crossing the Atlantic.

To serve 4

4 frozen cod steaks	4 small potatoes
4 slices back bacon	4 medium onions

1 tablesp. butter   salt and pepper
¼ pt milk

Wet the bottom of the saucepan, cut bacon into inch squares and drop them into the pan. Place fish on this and cover with water. Season with pepper and a little salt.

Slice potatoes thinly and add. Top finally with thinly sliced onions and boil slowly for half an hour. When cooked, add milk and butter. Heat through and serve (in soup plates to eat with a spoon is best).

from Nicole de Bedford, Duchess of Bedford
Scallops Meribel

With such a large, busy house as Woburn Abbey no one would ever think I had time to cook, but I do. Every Christmas we go to my little house at the top of a mountain at Meribel in the Savoie, France, which I call my 'place of resurrection', and where I come down to earth for a few weeks and do all the shopping and cooking. Each year I invent several new recipes, for the delight of my husband and children and for the despair of my waistline! When the herd of white rhinos arrived at Woburn, Richard Chipperfield, wanting to honour my name, christened the 10-ton female, Nicole. This sent me into peals of laughter, much to his dismay, when I asked: 'Have you called it after me because we have the same waistline?'

To serve 6

2 pkts frozen scallops   1 glass white wine
2 pkts frozen shrimps   6 small teasp. chopped shallot
1 large carrot   12 raw mushrooms
2 medium onions   mornay sauce made with the
bay leaf   liquor the scallops were cooked
pinch of thyme   in, a little butter, flour, and
pinch of dill   grated cheese
1 glass water

Unfreeze scallops and shrimps several hours in advance, in separate bowls, so that their juices will not be lost. Put scallops in a pan with their juices, add a glass of water and a glass of white wine, the carrot, the onions, the bay leaf, a pinch of thyme and one of dill if possible. Bring to the boil and leave to simmer for 10 minutes, no more.

Prepare a mornay sauce using the liquor the scallops were cooked in. The sauce should be of the consistency of mayonnaise.

In individual ovenware dishes, put a teaspoonful of finely chopped raw shallot and two or three raw mushrooms and add scallops and shrimps. Cover well with mornay sauce, put into a hot oven 425°F. Mark 7 on a low shelf and bake until golden brown.

from Elizabeth Goudge, Author

Fish salad

This is the easiest possible recipe but I send it because whenever I make it everyone asks for more – which cannot be said for everything I make! It is useful for hot-weather lunch parties and especially for lunch in the garden. With a little preparation the day before it can be made in a moment. White fish should be used – not salmon, and not smoked haddock, which awakes memories of heavy schoolroom kedgeree, and this dish should not taste in the least like kedgeree.

white fish
rice (equal quantity, when
    cooked, to fish)
1–2 carrots
1–2 hard-boiled eggs
capers

2 or more lemons, according to
    quantities cooked
chopped parsley
lettuce hearts
home-made salad dressing

Cook the fish, the carrots and the rice in the quantities required. The rice should be very dry. Next day, flake the fish and mix with an equal quantity of rice, one or two hard-boiled eggs chopped finely, chopped carrot and plenty of capers. Sprinkle over the mixture the juice of two lemons (or more if you are making a large quantity) and plenty of chopped parsley. Pile on a dish and surround with lettuce hearts.

Have in a glass jug plenty of home-made salad dressing. (Do not dare to use anything out of a bottle.) Do not pour it over the salad beforehand, for it should not be damp or heavy.

Vary this mixture in any way you like, provided you keep the capers and lemon juice, but this is the mixture I have found best.

from Charles Wintour, Editor of the London *Evening Standard*

Kedgeree

The best possible dish either for Sunday breakfast or supper. There are a variety of ways of doing it, but I think this, which originally appeared in the *Evening Standard*, is the best.

To serve 3–4

6 oz. long-grain rice
2 lb. smoked haddock
3–4 oz. butter
1 finely chopped onion

2 oz. shrimps
2 hard-boiled eggs
2–3 tablesp. single cream
parsley

Boil rice, drain and spread on a linen cloth to dry. Simmer haddock gently in water until soft. Remove skin and bones and flake fish into fairly small pieces.

Melt butter in a large saucepan and simmer onion in it until transparent. Add rice and flaked fish and turn over gently so as not to break the fish. Add shrimps (a small carton of frozen shrimps is easiest) and chopped egg whites, turn into a double boiler (or use a basin standing in a pan of hot water) and heat through. Add cream and turn out onto serving platter, sprinkling egg yolks (sieved) and chopped parsley on top.

Note: The double boiler is not essential but makes heating easier and allows the kedgeree to be made in advance and left until wanted.

from Clement Freud, Cookery Journalist, Television Personality

Salmon steaks (first published in the *Observer* Magazine)

salmon steaks
butter
salt and pepper
dry white wine

For the mousseline sauce:
3 egg yolks
1 teasp. lemon juice
6 oz. butter
¼ pt double cream

Place salmon steaks on a sheet of buttered foil, add salt and pepper, brush fish with melted butter, sprinkle with a dry white wine, cover with more foil and bake in a medium oven for 20–30 minutes. This will give you time to make a very beautiful mousseline sauce: 3 egg yolks and a teaspoon of lemon juice blended in a basin engaged over a pan of boiling water. Add 6 oz. melted butter, a spoonful at a time, whisking as the sauce thickens, then add to it a ¼ pt of lightly-beaten double cream and juices from the foil.

from Robert Nye, Novelist, Poet, Critic, and Playwright
Fish pie

This is tasty and economical, providing enough for me, my wife Aileen and our six children – Rebecca, Sharon, Jack, Malory, Owen and Taliesin. There is never any left over for sad Leonardo, our blue Persian cat.

To serve 8 or more

6 fillets of white fish	mixed herbs
flour	salt and pepper
bread	about ½ pt milk
tomatoes	cheese
butter	syboes (spring onions)

Dip the fillets in flour and place 2 in a suitably shaped oven-ware dish with lid. Season them with salt and pepper and almost cover them with a layer of bread – chunky bread rather than finely crumbed. Sprinkle mixed herbs over and top with thin slices of tomato and butter. Repeat in layers with the other fillets, topping the final layer with grated cheese.

Carefully pour about ½ pt milk down the sides of the dish to reach the bottom layer. Cook covered in a moderate oven 380°F. Mark 5 for ½–¾ hour. Remove the lid shortly before the pie is thoroughly cooked to allow the top layer of bread to crisp and the cheese to toast. Scatter chopped syboes over the hot pie and serve it with French fried potatoes cut in rounds, or chips, or anything else preferred.

from Sir Derek Jakeway, former Governor of Fiji Islands
Kokonda

To serve 4

½–1 lb. any thick white-fleshed fish	1 pt boiling water
	salt
8 oz. dessicated coconut	2–3 lemons

½ small sweet pepper   ½ carrot
2 chilli peppers   ½ tomato
½ small onion   2 oz. thick cream

Pour the boiling water on to the dessicated coconut and leave for 24 hours. Strain, and place in fridge to chill.

Skin, clean and bone the uncooked fish and cut into small cubes. Sprinkle with plenty of salt and pour on lemon juice. Press fish well into lemon juice and, stirring occasionally, leave for 2 hours.

Chop peppers and onion finely, scrape and grate carrot, remove seeds from tomato and cut up finely. Pour off lemon juice from the fish. Mix the cream into the coconut milk and add the mixture to the fish. Taste, and add some of the lemon juice if necessary. Put back in fridge and chill. Just before serving (in small individual glasses or glass bowls), add all the chopped vegetables and mix well.

POULTRY AND MEAT

from Athene Seyler, Actress

Marinaded chicken

A useful recipe when cooking for guests, as it can be left in the oven till required (guests late, or lingering over cocktails).

pieces of chicken, as required, or half poussins
butter
Marinade:
3 tablesp. olive oil

1 gill wine or cider
1 finely chopped onion
butter
3 cloves
salt and pepper

Leave the chicken in the marinade 1 hour, in a dish which will fit in the oven and serve direct to table – preferably enamelled iron.

Remove chicken and grill very brown on both sides with butter. Return to the marinade dish, cover with foil and cook in a low oven, 290°F, Mark 1, for an hour at least, if not longer. If the liquid needs adding to, put in some stock, but it should only be about an inch deep altogether. Very delicious flavour.

from Professor Fred Hoyle, Plumian Professor of Astronomy and Experimental Philosophy and Author of Science Fiction Books

Whole curried chicken with saffron rice (first published in *The Times*)

To serve 6

1 (4–5 lb.) oven-ready chicken
For the stuffing:
4 oz. long grain rice
1 oz. butter or margarine
1 small onion, finely chopped
1 level dessertsp. curry powder
½ level teasp. salt
For the curry sauce:
1½ oz. butter or margarine
1 small onion, finely chopped
3 level tablesp. curry powder
1 pt stock (use water and chicken stock cube)

1 rounded tablesp. plain flour
1 tablesp. mango chutney (chop up any large pieces)
1 rounded tablesp. soft brown sugar
juice of ½ lemon
½ level teasp. salt
For the saffron rice:
8 oz. long grain rice
pinch of saffron
pinch of granulated sugar
2 tablesp. almost boiling water

Wipe chicken, remove any bag of giblets and set aside while preparing stuffing. Add rice to boiling salted water, stir well, re-boil and cook rapidly for 8 minutes. Meanwhile melt butter in small pan, add onion and fry gently until soft. Stir in curry powder, then drained cooked rice and season with salt. Stir ingredients to blend, then spoon into body cavity of bird. Skewer chicken closed and place in large casserole dish.

Melt butter for curry sauce in medium saucepan, add onion and cook gently for 5–10 minutes until onion is soft. Stir in curry powder and cook for further 5 minutes to bring out flavours and oils. Then stir in the flour and gradually the stock. Bring to the boil and add the remaining ingredients. Cover and simmer gently for ½ hour, then strain sauce over chicken.

Cover casserole and place in centre of slow oven 310°F. Mark 2. Cook gently for 3–4 hours, basting occasionally. The longer the chicken cooks the better the flavour; in this particular recipe the chicken should be overcooked to the extent that it almost falls apart when served.

About 15 minutes before serving prepare saffron rice. Add rice to a saucepan of boiling salted water. Re-boil, stirring all the time and cook rapidly for 8–10 minutes. Strain and return to hot saucepan. Cover and keep warm. Rice is coloured yellow using an infusion of saffron. For this, grind a pinch of saffron and a pinch of granulated sugar to a fine powder. Then stir in hot water. Infuse for about 10 minutes, then strain into cooked rice. Mix until all grains are coloured. Serve chicken with sauce and rice.

from Sir Basil Spence, Architect
Poulet Simla

Although I do not cook, I am blessed with a wife who cooks very well indeed and this is one of my favourites.

To serve 4–6

1 chicken, freshly roasted	salt and pepper
½ pt whipped cream	boiled rice
1 teasp. mustard	1 teasp. dry curry
2 tablesp. Worcester sauce	A little chopped chutney

Cut up and arrange in a fireproof dish a freshly roasted chicken. To ½ pt stiffly whipped cream add 1 teasp. mustard, 2 tablesp. Worcester sauce, and salt and pepper. Pour this over the chicken and stand in a medium oven 380°F. Mark 5 till brown.

Serve with boiled rice flavoured with a teaspoonful of dry curry and a little chopped chutney.

from Arnold Wesker, Playwright
Cold curried chicken

To serve 4–6

1 hen boiled with salt and bay leaf until meat falls away from the bone	1 large carton double cream
	¼ pt mayonnaise (approx. according to taste)

2 tablesp. Madras curry powder
  (according to taste)
white sliced almonds

Danish-type caviar (or real
  caviar, according to pocket)
tinned pears

Peel meat from bone and spread chicken in centre of oval dish. Beat the cream until thick: mix with the mayonnaise. Stir in the Madras curry powder. Spread over chicken and sprinkle with the caviar, then with the sliced almonds. Decorate border with tinned pears. Serve cold.

P.S. With water from the chicken, add carrots, onions, tomatoes, turnips, celery and barley – boil twice and you have Chicken Soup with Barley.

from Julie Christie, Actress

Chicken with honey (1)

To serve 6

2 chickens, each sliced into three
  parts
1 large onion
6 oz. butter
6 dessertsp. honey

2–4 teasp. curry powder, according to taste
1 dessertsp. vinegar
cornflour

Slice the onion and fry gently in the butter in a large and deep casserole. Add the pieces of chicken, turning so that both sides are well buttered, put 1 dessertsp. of honey on each piece, and put on lid. Place in a very hot oven 500°F. Mark 10. After ¼ hour, baste and reduce heat to 350°F. Mark 4. Cook for about ½ hour more, basting twice. Remove pieces of chicken, keep hot, and add enough water to the juices in the casserole to make up to about ¾ pt stock.

In a cup, mix 2–4 teasp. curry powder with water. Add this to the stock together with the vinegar. Cook gently for a few minutes, and if necessary, thicken with cornflour. Taste and adjust seasonings. Put chicken pieces back, reheat and serve.

from Barbara Cartland, Author and Television Personality
Chicken with honey (2)

Being a great believer in health I think it is very important
to try and buy everything possible either from Health Stores or
from people who you know are not selling you food loaded with
chemicals. Here is a recipe which should be made with a chicken
that has not been caponized, and comes from a farm; being
cooked with honey, it is exceedingly good for everyone who eats
it.

1 farm chicken	2 lemons
2 oz. vegetable margarine or	a little rosemary
sunflower oil	parsley
4 tablesp. honey	

Cut up chicken and fry in margarine or oil. After quick browning, reduce heat, cover pan and cook for 25 minutes, turning
once. Make a sauce of the honey with the juice of 1 lemon and a
little rosemary.* Pour this over the chicken and baste for 2
minutes. Serve in a hot dish and garnish with parsley and slices
of lemon.

I find that a watercress and lettuce salad goes very well with
this. Lemon juice can also be squeezed over the chicken if
necessary.

* Don't overdo the rosemary – it's potent stuff. *Ed.*

from Robin Bailey, Actor
Chicken piri-piri

This is based on a Portuguese national dish.

To serve 6

6 good joints of chicken	herbs as available (thyme,
about ⅛ pt lemon juice	marjoram, basil, tarragon)
about ⅛ pt oil	pepper and salt

about 2 (they are very strong) hot red peppers (or the bottled green kind)

handful of raisins
small tin of cherries (optional)
rice

Marinate the chicken pieces for at least 1 hour (the longer the better) in equal quantities of oil and lemon juice – about ¼ pt altogether – to which have been added herbs, a good handful of raisins, pepper and salt and the hot peppers cut up small. Put chicken pieces into an ovenproof dish with some of the marinade, cover and cook in a medium oven 355°F. Mark 4, basting from time to time, for about 1 hour or until tender.

Serve on a bed of rice with some of the juice from the cooking poured over (reserve some and serve separately in case the flavour is too strong for some tastes). For added colour, you can pour a small tin of cherries heated in their juice, over all (but this would not be done in Portugal).

from Arthur Brittenden, Editor of the *Daily Mail*

First edition chicken

Usually eaten between 10.30 and 11.0 p.m. while waiting for the First Edition of the *Daily Mail*. Appetizing and not too stodgy or snacky. The idea originally came from a little Italian restaurant where Mrs Brittenden had gone in a panic because she had forgotten to order any meat. They immediately rustled up two chicken escalopes and promised they would be delicious. They were!

The hardest part about this recipe is preparing the escalopes, but once the surgery is over the rest is easy.

3 meaty chicken pieces	2 tablesp. butter
salt and pepper	a little lemon juice
tarragon or other favourite herb	

Remove the skin from the chicken pieces and then cut the flesh away from the bone. Try to keep it in one piece. Then place the chicken between two damp pieces of greaseproof paper and flatten them. They obviously won't be as see-through as veal escalopes, but that doesn't matter. Season with salt and pepper and any favourite herb like tarragon which goes beautifully with chicken.

Melt 2 tablesp. of butter in a heavy frying pan and cook chicken gently for 8–10 minutes. Remove chicken when cooked and keep warm. Add lemon juice – just a sprinkling – to the pan and increase heat. Pour hot butter and lemon over chicken. Garnish with a sprinkling of parsley.

Serve watercress and chicory salad with chicken. Cucumber cream goes well with this dish. Peel and de-seed half a cucumber, dice and add to melted butter in pan. Poach cucumber gently for five minutes. Add salt and pepper and some double cream.

New potatoes which have been cooked in their jackets and peeled before serving also go well with First Edition Chicken.

from Jean Metcalfe, Broadcaster
Savoury oven-fried chicken

To serve 4

1 tender 2½ lb. frying chicken, or joints	1 teasp. dried rosemary, crushed
	grated rind of 1 lemon
2 oz. flour	1 egg, beaten
1 teasp. salt	milk
½ level teasp. crushed black pepper	4 tablesp. butter
	4 tablesp. olive oil
1 tablesp. finely chopped parsley	thin triangles of bread
1 teasp. dried tarragon, crushed	

Cut chicken into serving pieces. Remove neck and back-bone and reserve for some other use. Combine flour, salt, pepper, parsley, tarragon, rosemary and grated lemon rind in a bowl. Combine beaten egg and a little milk in another bowl. Dip chicken pieces into egg mixture, then into seasoned flour. Chill. Place butter and oil in a shallow baking dish and heat in a moderately hot oven 400°F. Mark 6 until butter sizzles. Place chicken pieces in dish; spoon butter over them and cook for 45–50 minutes, or until chicken is tender and brown, turning once or twice during cooking. Serve on thin triangles of toast sautéed in butter, with green salad and French dressing.

from Rita Tushingham, Actress

Chicken casserole

To serve 8

8 chicken pieces with skin
  removed
2 medium onions, finely chopped
1 oz. butter
3 cloves garlic, crushed
1 level teasp. mixed herbs
salt and pepper

a little flour
6 peeled tomatoes, finely chopped
1 large tin mushroom soup
¼ lb. mushrooms, washed and
  quartered
4 carrots, finely chopped
¼ pt double cream

Fry the onions in butter till transparent, then add the tomatoes, garlic, mixed herbs, and salt and pepper to taste. Continue to fry for about 3 minutes, then add the mushroom soup, mix well and pour into a casserole dish. Add the mushrooms and carrots. Now dip the chicken pieces into seasoned flour and fry to seal (about 2 minutes on each side). Add to the casserole and stir; cook in a very slow oven 250°F. Mark $\frac{1}{4}$–$\frac{1}{2}$ for about 2 hours (after coming to simmering point) or until chicken is tender. Add the cream $\frac{1}{2}$ hour before serving.

from Elizabeth David, Writer of standard works on food and cooking

Chicken grilled with aromatic herbs

1 small roasting chicken weighing about $1\frac{1}{2}$–$1\frac{3}{4}$ lb. net weight (i.e. when plucked and dressed but including, usually, the weight of the giblets, which will be 3–4 oz.)

olive oil

dried tarragon, thyme, basil or marjoram

lemon juice

salt and freshly milled pepper

watercress

lemon quarters

First, if you are obliged to use a frozen bird, let it thaw out thoroughly. In my experience this takes pretty well all day in a warm kitchen. Secondly, don't forget, when the bird has thawed, that some frozen chickens have their giblets pushed back inside them in a bag and this must be taken out before you attempt to cut the chicken in half for grilling.

Once thawed it is quite easy to split a small chicken right down the back and through the breastbone with a sharp and heavy knife. But if you have no such utensil, ask the poulterer to do the job for you – that is, if you are buying fresh and not a frozen bird. Cut off also the extremity of the leg, up to the first joint.

All you have then to do is to put the halves in the grill pan, sprinkle both sides very generously with olive oil, lemon juice and dried herbs if you have them (tarragon is best; basil is also first class, thyme or marjoram good; sage and rosemary too overpowering; fresh herbs are unsuitable because they will burn). When feasible, leave the chicken pieces (covered) to steep for an hour or so. Just before starting to cook them rub both sides with salt and freshly milled pepper.

Start them off, skin side up, fairly near the grill. After about 7 minutes, turn them over and cook for about another 10 minutes, a little further away from the heat. Turn them skin side up again for a final 3 minutes or so.

Serve the grilled chicken on a well-heated dish, with all its juices, plenty of lemon quarters and tufts of watercress. With chicken grilled in this way vegetables are redundant, but a tomato salad makes the right contrast to the sizzling aromatic chicken.

from the Rt Rev. Mervyn Stockwood, Bishop of Southwark

Poulet évêque

To serve 6

1 4 lb. chicken	¾ oz. flour
1 oz. butter	¼ pt cider
2 oz. onion	½ pt good stock
2 sticks of celery, or 1 small leek	½ gill or more of cream
2 apples and another 2 for garnish	

Cut the chicken into joints. Flour lightly and sauté in the butter until golden brown. Remove from pan and put in finely chopped onion. Sauté gently for 4–5 minutes, then add sliced celery or leek, and two peeled and chopped apples. Sauté for another 5 minutes. Add the flour, cider and broth. Bring to the boil. Replace the pieces of chicken, cover and simmer until the meat is cooked and the sauce well flavoured.

Remove the chicken to a hot dish, strain the sauce, correct seasoning, return to a small pan and bring to the boil. Whisk in the cream. Pour sauce over the chicken pieces. Serve at once, garnished with fried apple rings.

from Margaret Leighton, Actress and Cook

Poulet à la Leighton with chive sauce

If you are cold and hungry, this should grab you!

To serve 4–8

2 4–5 lb. roasting chickens	2 teasp. salt
8 whole peeled carrots	*For chive sauce:*
1 head of celery	¾ lb. butter
4 large leeks (white parts only)	grated rind of 2 lemons
4 medium onions	salt and pepper to taste
6 peppercorns	pinch of nutmeg (optional)
1 small bay leaf	2 heaped tablesp. chopped chives

Peel and wash carrots, remove leaves from celery, clean and tie the sticks in a bundle. Remove green parts from leeks, split white parts down the centre, wash well, and make into a bundle. Peel the onions.

Wash chickens, dry and truss. Place side by side in an enamel pan and add just enough water to cover (not more than 3 qts). Place on low heat until water comes to boiling point, skim carefully, and add carrots, leeks, onions, celery, peppercorns and bay leaf. Simmer gently for one hour, then season with salt and continue simmering gently until tender but not falling apart. Turn the chickens once while cooking.

When done, remove from heat, lift chickens carefully from the broth and pull off as much skin as is possible without causing the birds to lose their shape. Place in a clean pan and strain the broth back over them. Keep hot until ready to serve, at which time place them on a hot platter. Remove strings. Carve the breast and loosen the joints, leaving the meat on the carcase. Garnish with parsley, surround birds with vegetables and serve accompanied by a bowl of chive and butter sauce, and small boiled potatoes. The soup should be served in cups and sipped whilst eating the chicken.

To make the chive sauce: first clarify the butter, letting it melt *very slowly* over a low flame. Skim off the froth as it rises to the surface, then pour off the clear butter into another pan, thus avoiding the sediment at the bottom. Just before serving the chickens, re-heat butter, add the grated rind of 2 lemons, a pinch of salt, a little freshly ground black pepper, a pinch of nutmeg if you like, and last of all, two heaped tablesp. of finely chopped chives.

from Michael and George, Restaurateurs, l'Epicure Restaurant, Soho, London

Chicken coronation

. . . so named because it was introduced to the menu in commemoration of coronation year. The pride of the dish is the sinfully rich sauce chasseur.

To serve 4

4 chicken breasts
butter
salt and pepper
dash of brandy
1 dessertsp. double cream
For the stock:
bones of chicken
1 small onion
1 carrot
1 stick celery
bouquet garni

For the sauce chasseur:
1 onion
1 carrot
1 stick celery
2 oz. butter
2 tablesp. flour
1 dessertsp. tomato purée
1 glass red wine
½ pt stock made from chicken
    bones
pinch of mixed herbs (optional)
¼ lb. mushrooms

Remove the skin from the chicken breasts (pull from the wing and it will come off the breastbone easier). Make about ½ pt stock.

To make the sauce: chop, not too finely, onion, carrot and celery. Place in frying pan with the butter and flour and fry slowly to a golden brown. Add the tomato purée, the wine and the stock, stirring gently with wooden spoon. Simmer gently for 30 minutes.

Now strain into a saucepan, add sliced mushrooms and simmer for 20 minutes at a very low heat. Add salt and pepper to taste. A pinch of mixed herbs may also be added at this stage if desired.

Sprinkle the chicken breasts with salt and pepper and fry in butter – in a frying pan – for approximately 7–8 minutes, until golden brown on both sides. Add a good dash of brandy and flambé the chicken. Add the sauce and simmer gently for two minutes. Finally, add 1 dessertsp. fresh double cream, and sprinkle with chopped parsley.

from Maître Chef Mérard, of Gleneagles Hotel, Perthshire

Caneton Montreuil

To serve 4

1 medium sized young duck	clear stock (or water)
root vegetables:	small can of peach caps
1 large carrot	2 tablesp. brown sugar
1 large onion	arrowroot or cornflour
1 large potato	cherries
2 half glasses brandy	garden peas
salt and pepper	

First prepare the duck for the oven by removing neck, wing and leg extensions thus leaving the bird ready for the table when halved; skewer as necessary.

Set the oven to 300°F. Mark 1–2. Arrange in the bottom of a suitably sized casserole ½ inch thick slices of the root vegetables as a bed for the bird. Cover these roots with a clear stock or seasoned water to which should be added a half glass of brandy, place the seasoned bird thereon, together with the extremities, cover with the lid and set to cook. Test the duck after ¾ hour and remove if tender, leaving the extremities, the bed of roots and the liquor in the casserole. Portion the duck and sprinkle with the brown sugar before placing under the grill to brown. Reserve in a warm place while the sauce is made.

Add the syrup from the tin of peaches to the cooking liquor and roots, simmer for a few moments, then strain off into a saucepan and add arrowroot or cornflour to thicken. Ensure that the thickening agent has thoroughly cooked into the sauce before adding the second half glass of brandy.

Place the cooked duck on an entrée dish and mask it with the sauce. Dress with the halved peach caps previously heated, topping each with a cherry. Dress the circumference of the dish with garden peas.

from Elizabeth Ray, Cookery Writer

Boeuf à la mode

We are very much a 'cold-food' family, liking all kinds of pâtés, charcuterie and salads, and this beef dish is a great favourite. Ideally it should be made with a calf's foot to make the jelly, but these are not easy to come across, so two pig's trotters can be used instead.

a piece of lean beef such as topside	red or white wine
a little fat	1 bay leaf
1 lb. onions	1 sprig thyme
3–4 carrots	salt and pepper
1 clove garlic	1 calf's foot or 2 pig's trotters

Season the piece of beef and brown well on all sides in the fat. Put it into a casserole with a lid. Sauté the sliced onions until golden (the same fat can be used) together with the carrots, sliced. Add these to the meat in the casserole with a crushed clove of garlic, the bay leaf, thyme, and salt and pepper. Split the calf's foot or trotters and place these on top or round the meat, and cover the whole with half wine and half water. Put the lid on the casserole and cook in a slow oven 250°F. Mark ¼–½ for 5–6 hours. If you have a timer on the oven it can stay in all night without coming to harm.

When cooked, remove the meat from the casserole and cool it under a light weight, which makes it easier to slice. Slice it thinly when cold and pour over it the strained and de-fatted liquid which will set to a delicious soft jelly. The carrots can be used as garnish if desired.

from Simon Dee, Television Personality
Roast lamb with apricot sauce

To serve 6–8

1 leg of lamb (approx. 4 lb.)	2 tablesp. wine
1 clove garlic (optional)	dash of vinegar
2 oz. lard or bacon fat	1 tablesp. brown sugar
salt and pepper	1 oz. butter
For the apricot sauce:	pinch each cinnamon and nutmeg
1 can (15½ oz.) apricots	

Wipe leg of lamb with damp cloth, rub over with a cut clove of garlic if liked, and spread with lard or bacon fat. Sprinkle with salt and pepper. Place in roasting tin and cover with foil. Put into pre-heated moderately hot oven 375°F. Mark 5 and allow 30 minutes per pound.

To prepare sauce: pass the apricots through a sieve or liquid-izer to make a smooth purée. Turn into a pan, add vinegar, sugar, butter and spices. Heat gently for 10–15 minutes, stirring frequently. Serve hot.

from John Arlott, Writer and Broadcaster
Loin of lamb with béarnaise sauce

To serve 4–5

one loin of lamb boned and rolled (the butcher will do this)	½ teasp. tarragon
For the sauce:	½ teasp. chervil
1 shallot (or equivalent amount of chopped onion)	2 tablesp. wine vinegar
	2 egg yolks
	3 oz. melted butter

Roast the lamb in a medium oven (375°F. Mark 5) for about 1 hour.

Put the chopped shallot, tarragon, chervil and vinegar in the top half of a double saucepan and reduce the vinegar by about half. Allow to cool slightly and add the beaten egg yolks. Put the pan over the bottom of the double saucepan full of hot water (or use a basin standing in a pan of hot water) and beat until the egg cooks sufficiently to thicken; then, still beating, add the butter slowly until it is all absorbed and the sauce is the consistency of custard. Strain and finish with a sprinkle of chopped tarragon.

The classic béarnaise sauce is always made with tarragon, but a very pleasant variation to accompany the lamb can be made using chopped mint and chives instead. Care must be taken to avoid making the sauce too hot or it may separate or scramble: it should be served warm, not hot. If it does separate it can be reconstituted by whisking in a few drops of cold water.

When ready to serve, carve the lamb into slices about 1 inch thick. Hand the sauce separately. An ideal accompaniment is a dish of fresh summer vegetables – peas, young carrots, broad beans.

from Kenneth Williams, Actor
Steak and kidney

To serve 4

1 lb. rump steak
½ lb. kidney
salt and pepper

¾ pt stock (packet vegetable soup)

I get a pound of rump steak and half a pound of kidney from the butcher, expressly saying 'NO FAT', and then put the lot into a casserole dish with seasoning and ¾ pt stock generally made out of one of those vegetable packet soups, and cook in the oven on low heat, 290°F. Mark 1, for about 3 to 4 hours. Served with mashed potatoes – they soak up the gravy. The whole thing is delicious and takes a minimum amount of time.

from Victor Silvester, Bandleader and Dancer
Steak à la Silvester

1 fillet steak per person
flour
salt and pepper
2 oz. butter (or 1 oz. butter, 1 oz. dripping)

½ teasp. French mustard
chopped parsley
Worcester sauce
½ clove garlic, crushed (optional)

Beat steaks flat and sprinkle with seasoned flour. Melt the fat in a pan, stirring in the mustard, a little chopped parsley and a dash of Worcester sauce, and the garlic if desired. Place steaks in pan and cook about 1½ minutes each side. Serve with creamed potatoes and green peas.

from Eugène Kaufeler, Maître Chef des Cuisines, The Dorchester Hotel, London
Côtelettes Sir Robert

lamb cutlets
salt and pepper

flour
egg

breadcrumbs
butter
cream sauce, i.e. white sauce with
   the addition of cream

button mushrooms
shallots
asparagus tips

Season and flour the cutlets, dip in egg and cover with bread-crumbs. Fry in butter until cooked.

Make a cream sauce and add some sliced button mushrooms and a little shallot which have previously been lightly fried. Put the sauce on to a dish and serve the cutlets on top. Garnish with asparagus tips.

from Michael J. Fish (Mr Fish), Mayfair Designer and Sartorial Artist

English lamb chops

To serve 5–6

10–12 lamb chops
⅔ cup tomato sauce
⅔ cup vinegar
⅓ cup Worcestershire sauce
1 onion, grated

1 teasp. dry mustard
1 teasp. salt
1 teasp. garlic salt
fat to fry chops

Combine the tomato sauce, vinegar, Worcestershire sauce, onion, mustard and salts in a bowl. Mix well. Marinate the chops in this at room temperature for 1 hour.

Drain, reserving the sauce. Pan fry the chops, turning frequently until done. Heat the sauce in a separate saucepan and pour over the chops. Serve with boiled rice and mixed vegetables.

from the Hon. Mrs Bratza, widow of the distinguished violinist

Porc citroné

To serve 4

4 pork chops	4 tablesp. demerara sugar
dripping	2 tablesp. water
lemon	salt and pepper
4 tablesp. tomato ketchup	

Brown the chops in the dripping on one side, turn and lay a slice of lemon on the top. Brown the other side.

In a bowl, mix the tomato ketchup, the demerara sugar and the water. Spoon this over the chops, cover and simmer for 30 minutes, basting occasionally with the sauce. After 30 minutes, remove cover and simmer for another 10 minutes. Serve with mashed potatoes and a green salad.

from The Rt Hon. Edward Heath, Prime Minister

Veal with orange stuffing

To serve 4–5

	For the stuffing:
1½ lb. veal steak	6 tablesp. soft breadcrumbs
made mustard	½ level tablesp. herbs
flour	grated rind of an orange
salt and pepper	½ beaten egg
fat for frying	salt and pepper
stock	

Divide the veal into 8 or 10 even-sized oblong pieces. Mince any trimmings and add to stuffing. Lightly spread veal with made mustard and with stuffing. Roll up and fix with fine string or wooden sticks.

Dip the rolls in seasoned flour and brown a little in hot fat. Place in casserole and add stock. Cook slowly in centre of warm oven 300°–325°F. Mark 2–3, for about 45–60 minutes. Serve with rice and chopped peppers.

from The Most Rev. and Rt Hon. A. M. Ramsay, Archbishop of Canterbury
Burgundy beef

To serve 4

1½ lb. shoulder or chuck steak	*For marinade:*
3 oz. streaky bacon	1 large onion sliced
6 baby onions (or shallots)	¼ pt Burgundy
1 oz. dripping	2 tablesp. olive oil
1½ tablesp. flour	*For garnish:*
4 oz. mushrooms	1 dozen baby onions
1 pt stock	a few whole baby carrots
salt and pepper	3 oz. mushrooms
thyme, parsley and a little celery	parsley
seed tied in muslin	butter or bacon fat

Cut the beef into 1½ inch squares, removing all fat. Sprinkle with salt and pepper, cover with sliced onion and pour over the wine and oil. Leave to marinate 3–6 hours. Then drain well.

Cut bacon into thin strips and fry in the dripping. Set aside. Fry baby onions gently in the same dripping until slightly coloured, set aside with bacon and brown the well-drained pieces of meat in the same dripping, sprinkling in the flour to absorb excess fat. Remove from heat, pour in the marinade, add bacon and onions, herbs and washed and sliced mushrooms. Add the stock, turn all into a warmed casserole and cook in the oven at low heat 310°F. Mark 2 for 2½ hours after reaching simmering point.

Meanwhile, lightly fry the extra mushrooms whole in a little butter or bacon fat; cook the carrots and extra baby onions together in a little slightly salted water until just tender, then drain well. Remove the herbs from the casserole, put in the onions and the mushrooms and cook for a further half hour, making 2½ hours in all. Serve sprinkled with chopped parsley.

from Raymond Gower, Master British Cook at Simpson's-in-the-Strand

Steak, kidney and mushroom pudding (with oysters)

This is Simpson's old and famous recipe.

To serve 4

1½ lb. lean beef	milled black pepper
½ lb. kidney	a little cold stock, or water
4 oz. onions	*For the suet paste:*
4 oz. mushrooms	1 lb. flour
12 oysters	½ teasp. salt
1 oz. flour	1 teasp. baking powder
1 teasp. salt	10 oz. chopped beef suet
1 tablesp. chopped parsley	¼ pt cold water

Make the suet paste first. Sieve flour, salt and baking powder, mix in the suet finely chopped, add cold water to make firm dough, allow to rest.

Cut meat and kidney into ¾ inch cubes, peel and chop the onion, wash and slice the mushrooms, place all in a bowl with the seasoning, chopped parsley and flour and mix together.

Butter a basin (about 7″), divide the paste into two, roll out one piece and line the basin, fill up with meat and add cold stock or water to come barely to the top of the meat. Arrange the oysters on top of the meat.

Roll out the other piece of paste to the size of the basin, cover and seal the top. Cover this with buttered greaseproof paper and a pudding cloth securely tied, and steam for four hours.

from Kenneth Allsop, Writer and Television
Commentator
Steak and kidney pie

Not really having a profound interest in food (all I demand is
that it should be superb) my life-of-the-table is pursued under
the illusion that I am a plain, simple man enjoying plain, simple
food. When I asked my wife to jot down how she prepared the
steak and kidney pie she serves up, I vaguely assumed that it
would be a rough peasant dish, probably cooked on hot stones
in a yard somewhere beyond my writing room. I was surprised
to see how subtly complicated it is – but its deliciousness is
consonant. What bestows distinction upon a steak and kidney
pie produced in the following way is (a) that it contains more
kidney than the normal skimpy rations allocated to steak and
kidney pies, and (b) the slow cooking of the meat extracts its full
flavour.

To serve 4–5

½ lb. short crust pastry	a little fat
1 medium-sized onion	1½ oz. flour
1 lb. chuck steak	seasoning
¾ lb. kidney	little red wine

Fry sliced onion gently for a few minutes in enough fat to cover
bottom of heavy-bottomed saucepan. Remove excess fat from
meat and cut rest of meat into small cubes (about ¾ inch).
Remove any skin and fat from kidneys, and cut up. Shake meat
and kidney in bag of about 1½ oz. seasoned flour. Turn up heat
under pan and cook meat for about a minute on each side. Add
small glass of red wine. Reduce heat and add remaining flour,
stirring well. Cook for a minute or two. Just cover with water,
bring to boiling and simmer for 2 hours. If liquid becomes too
thick, add a little more water.

Put steak and kidney in pie dish with liquor, cover with pastry,
make small hole in pastry to allow steam to escape, and cook for
about half an hour, or until pastry is lightly browned, in a fairly
hot oven pre-heated to 400°F. Mark 6.

from J. Porta, Chef de Cuisine, Stone's Chop House
Shepherd's pie

To serve 4

1 lb. cooked lamb or mutton	¼–½ pt thickened gravy
1½ oz. fat	1 lb. potatoes
4 oz. onions	2 oz. butter
salt and pepper	milk

Sweat the finely chopped onion in the fat without allowing it to colour. Mince the meat, from which all fat and gristle has been removed, and add to the onion. Season and add sufficient gravy to bind. Bring to the boil and simmer for 10–15 minutes, then place in pie dish or earthenware dish.

Prepare the mashed potatoes with the butter and a little milk. Arrange neatly on top of the meat, brush with milk and colour lightly under the grill or in hot oven.

N.B. Cooked meats should always be thoroughly reheated.

from Katherine Whitehorn, Journalist
Barbecued meat balls

Meat Balls: get them out of a tin or:	*Sauce:*
	2 onions
½ lb. veal mince	a little dripping or oil
½ lb. beef mince	3 tablesp. chilli sauce
1 egg	2 tablesp. vinegar
salt and pepper	½ teasp. paprika
1 tablesp. flour	a good shake Worcester sauce
deep fat for frying	a large squeeze tomato paste or 1 small size tin

Make the meat balls: mix veal and beef mince, bind with egg, roll in seasoned flour and fry in deep fat until brown.

For the sauce: fry the onions in a little dripping or oil, add chilli sauce, vinegar, paprika, Worcester sauce, tomato paste – and simmer 20 minutes. Put this over the meat balls and cook at least ¼ hour in a preheated moderate oven 380°F. Mark 5. If it all seems to be getting a bit dry, just add a little water and give it a good stir. Serve with rice and/or green salad.

Warning: it is pretty fiery; you can cut down the chilli sauce part if you like.

from Douglas Bader, Aviator
Cottage pie

fresh mince	flour
water	1 tablesp. tomato sauce
salt and pepper	dash Worcester sauce
2 medium onions	creamed potatoes
a little fat	butter

Simmer the mince with water to cover for 30 minutes, adding seasoning. Fry the onions, sliced, in a little fat until golden brown. Add a sprinkling of flour, tablesp. tomato sauce and a dash of Worcester sauce. Finally, the mince and stock should be added. This should come out fairly firm. Cover with creamed potatoes which should have small dabs of butter added on top. Brown lightly under the grill.

from Arthur Worsley, Ventriloquist
Dutch roast

¼ lb. minced beef	Worcester sauce
¼ lb. sausage meat	pinch of herbs
1 oz. dripping	salt and pepper
1 large onion	1 egg
2 oz. breadcrumbs	

Put the dripping in a roasting tin and place in a hot oven 425°F. Mark 7.

Put the meats in bowl, chop onion finely and add with bread-crumbs, seasoning, herbs and 1 teasp. Worcester sauce. Mix well, then add beaten egg. Turn the mixture out on to a floured board, form into a roll and put into the hot fat, basting well. Cook for 1 hour, basting from time to time.

from Arthur Askey, Comedian

Lancashire hot pot (1)

Something simple like myself. The recipe is for four but I intend eating it all myself. My favourite dish is really tripe – but I talk so much tripe in my act, it makes me feel like a cannibal when I eat it!

To serve 4

1 lb. best end of neck of mutton	salt and pepper
4–5 medium onions	a little dripping
2 lb. potatoes	

Trim fat off meat, peel and slice onions, peel potatoes and cut into thick slices. Put alternate layers of potatoes, onions and meat in a deep earthenware pot or dish, seasoning well between layers. The final layer must be potatoes and they should be stood on end. Add cold water but do not cover top layer of potatoes, which should be dabbed with a little dripping.

Put lid on pot, or cover with foil or greased paper. Bake in a moderate oven 380°F. Mark 5 about 2½ hours. For the last ½ hour, remove cover and raise heat a little to enable potatoes to become brown and slightly crisp.

from Frank Allaun, M.P.

Lancashire hot pot (2)

My favourite recipe is Lancashire Hot Pot. As you will under-stand, in food matters I am merely an expert at the receiving end and not at the producing end but my wife, who really does understand these things, says: this dish is traditional, plain, honest-to-God Lancashire cooking, which is becoming a rarity these days. When even the 'Chippies' are serving chow mein, curry, and sweet and sour pork – and country holidays mean continental cookery (which I am by no means knocking) a few of the good old-fashioned dishes 'mother used to make' come as a piquant and refreshing change. This dish is guaranteed to make one undo one's top button and have another helping, especially on a cold winter's night.

2 lb. mutton chops	3–4 kidneys
1 lb. onions	salt and pepper
2 lb. potatoes	2 oz. butter
8 oz. mushrooms	½ pt water
2 oz. bacon or ham	

Peel and slice onions, potatoes and mushrooms. Cut ham and kidneys into small pieces. Place a layer of chops in casserole, then mushrooms, ham, kidneys, onions and potatoes in layers, seasoning every layer. The last layer should be potatoes. Pour water over, place knobs of butter over potatoes, place lid on casserole and cook in slow oven 310°F. Mark 2 for about 3 hours. Just before serving, remove lid from casserole and brown potatoes in hot oven.

   Important: seasoning each layer and crisping and browning top layer of potatoes. Verdict: fit for a king.

from Dr Ronald Hill, Marathon Runner

Hot pot

This is the sort of dish it is nice to come home to after a cold, wet, cross-country race.

1 lb. lean braising steak	2 onions
6 medium-sized potatoes	1 tablesp. salt

Peel and slice the potatoes and onions. Place in layers in a deep casserole dish, starting with potatoes, then meat, then onions, and ending with a layer of potatoes. Add the salt, then add water to half-way up the dish. Place in a moderate oven 350°F. Mark 4 with the lid on, for 2 hours 20 minutes. Remove the lid and cook for 10 more minutes to brown the top layer.

This should be served with pickled red cabbage and 'mushy' peas (dried peas, soaked, then boiled until mushy).

from Bob Monkhouse, Entertainer

Carbonnades de boeuf

Hope you enjoy it as much as I do!

To serve 4

2 lb. chuck steak	4 lb. onions
salt and black pepper	1 tablesp. flour
2 tablesp. olive oil	1 bottle Guinness
2 tablesp. butter	

Heat olive oil in thick-bottomed frying pan. Season beef to taste with salt and black pepper, brown on both sides in oil, and place in flameproof casserole. Add butter to frying pan, and brown the onions, thinly sliced. Sprinkle with flour and add to meat in casserole. Add Guinness to cover, place lid on casserole and cook over low flame for about 2 hours or until beef is tender. Serve with creamed potatoes or noodles.

from Marcel Hoeffler, Restaurant Manager, Ritz Hotel, London

Queue de boeuf paysanne

Monsieur Marcel has, from time to time, suggested to his very distinguished clientèle many exotic dishes, but he himself prefers something simple. This is a dish he would prepare for his family and himself when he is at home.

1 or 2 oxtails
a little dripping
small piece of pork rind, diced
small piece raw ham, diced
flour
salt and pepper
a little red wine

a little white stock
carrots
turnips
shallots or small onions
new potatoes
butter

Cut the oxtail in pieces and fry lightly in a very little dripping, together with the dice of pork rind and raw ham and a few of the vegetables, cut small. Sprinkle in a little flour, season and moisten with red wine and white stock in about equal quantities. (The liquid should come about half-way up the meat and vegetables – not cover them.)

Cover tightly and cook very slowly for about 3½ hours, or more.

Fry some diced carrots and turnips and some shallots lightly in butter, and boil some new potatoes. When the oxtail is nearly ready, remove the pieces into another pan, add the diced carrots and turnips and the new potatoes. Strain the stock over the lot and finish cooking. Serve in a casserole.

from Sir Alec Rose, Round-the-World Yachtsman

Casserole of pork

To serve 4

1½ lb. loin of pork
1 oz. dripping
2 small onions
¾ lb. apples
1 oz. flour

¾ pt stock
pepper and salt
a little mustard
4 cloves

Divide the meat into chops, melt the dripping in a frying pan, peel and slice the onions and apples to form rings and fry until golden brown. Remove, and fry the chops. Remove chops from pan and stir in the flour adding a little more dripping if necessary. Cook the flour until it is nicely browned, stir in the stock, bring to boiling point and add the seasoning and a little mustard.

Place the chops in a casserole, cover with the fried apple and onion, pour over the prepared gravy. Cover with a lid and cook in a slow oven 310°F. Mark 2 for about 1½ hours.

from Julie Felix, Singer

Bulldog gravy

To serve 3–4

½–¾ lb. cooked beef*	1 teacup patna rice
2 large Spanish onions	wineglass of inexpensive red
2 large green peppers	wine
2 large aubergines	salt and pepper
2 large courgettes	paprika pepper
1½ lb. tomatoes	cayenne pepper
large can tomato purée	2 oz. butter
3 oz. mushrooms	1 tablesp. oil

Melt butter and heat oil in a saucepan, add the peeled and thinly sliced onions and gently fry until they are soft. Cut the aubergines, courgettes and peppers (having removed the seeds) into thick slices and add to the onions. Slice tomatoes and mushrooms, add to the pan, together with the tomato purée. Stir in the wine and rice, add salt, pepper, cayenne and paprika to taste, and stir again.

Put a lid on the pan and cook over a low heat for about ¾ hour, or until the vegetables and rice are cooked. Cut the cooked beef into cubes and add to the pan ¼ hour before serving.

* This meal cooked without meat is delicious for vegetarians.

from Irene Handl, Actress and Author
Tripes à la mode de Caen

You either like tripe or you don't, but many of the 'don'ts' have been converted by this dish.

To serve 3

butter	½ teasp. carraway seeds
1 large onion	salt and freshly ground pepper
2 lb. tripe	2 teasp. Marmite, Oxo or 2 cubes
1 pig's trotter	beef extract
1 bay leaf	

Melt a good piece of butter and fry in it the onion cut in thin slices until transparent but not brown. Meanwhile wash the tripe, roll up and cut into fine strips; and split the pig's trotter in half. Put all the meat into a saucepan with the fried onion; add a bay leaf, carraway seeds, salt and freshly ground black pepper, and Marmite or other extract. Bring gently to boiling point and simmer for a good 2 hours.

The amount of Marmite can be halved if desired but it should be enough to make a strong gravy. Do not on any account add water; there is sufficient moisture from washing the tripe and from drippings from the pan lid during simmering to give ample gravy, which should be clear but thick flowing because of the trotter. Stir from time to time to prevent sticking but if the meat should stick during the cooking process, by all means add a little boiling water.

When cooked, the tripe should be an appetizing golden-brown with just enough gravy to serve with every portion. Serve very hot in the pan it was cooked in (if this is a cast-iron casserole) or on heated deep dish with creamy mashed potatoes and a tossed green salad.

from Edward Lucie-Smith, Poet and Art Critic

Kebabs – Persian style

I like kebabs and I love yoghourt. This recipe combines the two.
The combination of meat and yoghourt is characteristic of Central
Asia – you find it again in Mutton Moghlai, the yoghourt and
mutton curry which the Moguls brought to India.

a shoulder of lamb, boned	1 large onion
2 large or 4 small cartons yoghourt	salt and pepper
½ teasp. crushed coriander (I put more – others may be more cautious)	rice
	cardamom seeds
	tomatoes and onions for salad

Cut up lamb into chunks 2 inches square, free of skin, sinew,
etc. Place in a marinade made of the yoghourt, the onion chopped
fine and the coriander. Leave in a bowl for 6–12 hours, stirring
occasionally. Do not refrigerate unless the weather is very hot,
but leave at room temperature, covered with a cloth.

Take lamb chunks from mixture, wipe or shake off marinade,
salt and pepper them and thread loosely on to skewers. Grill,
turning skewers so that the meat is done on all sides (10 minutes
or less). The meat should be just faintly pink when cut. Serve
with rice cooked with a few cardamon seeds for extra flavour,
plus a tomato and onion salad.

The marinade bleaches and tenderizes the meat; it should have
a very delicate, peppery flavour. The point about threading the
meat *loosely* rather than packing it tightly on the skewer is that
the metal of the skewer heats up and helps to cook the interior of
the chunks.

from Marceau Francoul, Maître Chef des Cuisines,
Claridge's, London

Curried lamb

To serve 4

2 lb. lamb (cutlets, or leg cut into cubes)	salt and pepper
	2 oz. curry powder

2 large onions, finely chopped
2 cloves garlic, chopped
4 oz. butter
2 oz. plain flour

4 tomatoes, peeled, pipped and
  chopped
3 oz. mango chutney, chopped
1 pt stock

Season the lamb with salt and pepper and sprinkle the curry
powder on top. Lightly fry the onions and garlic in butter
without colouring them. Add the lamb and curry powder and
cook slowly on top of the stove until lightly cooked. Add the
flour and place in a hot oven for a few minutes. Remove from
the oven and add the tomatoes and chutney. Add the stock
gradually, stirring continuously and bring to the boil. Check for
seasoning and cook lamb until tender.

from Robert Carrier, Cookery Writer and Restaurateur

Daube in the ashes

Can either be cooked in the ashes for a barbecue or outdoor
meal or just as easily cooked in the oven in the kitchen.

To serve 4–6

3 lb. shin of beef, cut into 2 in.
  cubes
1 lb. unsmoked bacon, in one
  piece
3 Spanish onions, sliced
3 tablesp. olive oil
3 tablesp. butter
flour

coarse salt
freshly ground black pepper
1–2 cloves garlic
1 strip dried orange peel
2 cloves
bouquet garni (2 sprigs thyme, 4
  sprigs parsley, 2 bay leaves)

Dice unsmoked bacon into large cubes; combine with sliced
onions, olive oil and butter, and sauté in a heatproof casserole
until onions are transparent. Sprinkle beef, cut into 2 inch
cubes, with flour; add to casserole and continue to cook, stirring
constantly, until beef browns. Then add coarse salt and freshly
ground black pepper, garlic, dried orange peel, cloves and

bouquet garni. Place a thick soup plate filled with cold water on top of the casserole to close it hermetically and place casserole in centre of hot ashes (bringing ashes up around casserole) for 2½–3 hours, replacing water in the soup plate as necessary.

For home cooking; place casserole in a preheated, very slow oven 270°–290°F. Mark ½–1 for 2½–3 hours.

from Pat Moss Carlsson, Rally Driver

Rabbit stewed in red wine

My father is a big breeder of rabbits, therefore we eat rabbit fairly often.

To serve 3–4

1 rabbit cut in pieces	1 lb. carrots (if liked) sliced
2 tablesp. olive oil	1 tablesp. flour
2 oz. butter	½–1 bottle cheap red wine
2 slices streaky bacon, cut ¼ in. thick	salt and pepper
about 15–20 pickling onions	3–4 bay leaves and a sprig of thyme

Melt butter, add oil, heat and then fry the bacon which should be cut into small slices. Add onions and carrots and fry for about 5 minutes. Remove, and fry rabbit pieces until lightly browned, add flour and cook for 1 minute, add wine and the bacon, carrots and onions, season with salt and pepper and bring to the boil. Put in bay leaves and thyme, reduce heat to a simmer and cook for about 1 hour or until tender. Remove herbs and serve. Potatoes can also be added to the dish if required.

from Raymond Postgate, Historian and Expert on Wine and Food

Ancient Roman ham

This recipe probably dates from immediately after the reign of Augustus Caesar. In one or two places the Latin is a little obscure, but I think that I have got it all right. Apicius, the distinguished gourmet who wrote it down, never gave times of cooking and these you must work out for yourself. It's not difficult.

a ham	Greek honey
a great many dried figs	pastry (short)
3 bay leaves	

Take a ham and boil it with a great many dried figs and 3 bay leaves. When it is nearly done take it out and strip the skin off. Make criss-cross cuts upon the outside and fill these with Greek honey. Wrap the whole joint in pastry – probably short and not puff pastry – and bake it in an oven. When the pastry is done, take the whole thing out and serve it as it is.

VEGETABLE DISHES

from The Rt Hon. Barbara Castle, M.P.

Marrow with cheese

An attractive way of doing marrow which makes a light supper dish.

1 marrow
1 large onion
2 tablesp. oil
2 oz. butter
tomato purée

1 dessertsp. basil
small pinch thyme
salt and pepper
sugar
parmesan cheese

Peel marrow and cut into cubes 1 inch square. Finely chop onion and soften slowly in a heavy frying pan in the oil and butter, until golden. Add the marrow cubes, the basil, thyme, a very large squeeze from a tube of tomato purée (or about a tablespoonful from a tin), salt, pepper and a little sugar. Cook until soft. Add a good quantity of grated parmesan cheese ten minutes before end.

from Joyce Grenfell, Writer, Entertainer

Sliced tomatoes

As a side salad or as an appetizer.

firm tomatoes	*For French dressing:*
salt and pepper	caster sugar
caster sugar	garlic vinegar
French dressing	olive oil
fresh mint	salt and black pepper

Peel and slice tomatoes and put them flat in an open dish. Lightly salt and pepper and then drop a little caster sugar (from a tea spoon) on to each slice and follow this with a drop (only) of French dressing. Top with finely chopped fresh mint.

The French dressing I make is kept in a jam jar with a screw-top lid. I mix it straight into the jar and do it all by eye measuring – first 2 inches of caster sugar; then about $1\frac{1}{2}$ inches of garlic vinegar; lastly, about an inch of olive oil, with pinch of salt and black pepper. Shake and stir well and store in a cool place.

from Benny Hill, Comedian

Salade niçoise

My favourite meals are taken outdoors in some Mediterranean country and some of my favourite foods originate in those areas. A salade niçoise can be made from a variety of ingredients but it always contains black olives, tomatoes and anchovies.

lettuce	wine vinegar
tomatoes	salt and pepper
small amount of red, green or	optional:
yellow sweet pepper	radishes, raw grated carrot,
a few black olives	celery, spring onions, young
a few anchovies	raw broad beans, hard-boiled
1 clove garlic	egg according to taste and
olive oil	season

Wash and dry the lettuce well. Slice the tomatoes, shred the pepper fairly small. Crush a clove of garlic and rub it well round the salad bowl, then discard what is left.

Make a rather oily French dressing, put lettuce, shredded pepper, radishes or any other hard ingredients such as celery or young, raw broad beans, into the bowl and dress, tossing well. Add tomatoes, olives and anchovies and turn the salad in the dressing again lightly. It must look fresh and crisp when served and not a soggy mess of crushed vegetables. Quarters of hard-boiled egg may be added – and sometimes tinned tunny fish is mixed in if a more substantial salad is required.

from Edwin Mullins, Journalist, Art Critic and Author

Sprouted beans

I don't cook if I can help it, though I like to toy with the idea that I would be fantastically good at it if I had to. I much prefer to keep it as something magical. If a cookery book were really able to put across to me the secret of a great dish, I should deeply suspect it.

Sprouted beans are said to pack an incredible amount of vitamins, but what I like about them is their fresh, crisp bite. The best and easiest beans to sprout are called Mung and can be bought at Indian grocers and Health Food Stores. The other things you need are half a yard of scalded cloth, such as butter muslin, and a shallow pie-dish.

Method: soak two handfuls of beans overnight in a bowl, and rinse them next morning in a sieve under the cold tap. Then wrap them in an envelope of cloth and put them into the pie-dish, keeping them damp but not standing in water, for 3–7 days. Rinse them under the cold tap 3–4 times daily, using the cloth to hold back the beans while you run the water off. (The resulting bright green liquid can be used for soup-stock.)

Sprouted beans can be eaten as soon as the curly sprouts begin to show, or at any time until the shoots begin to go brown. They keep well covered in the fridge, but will not grow further there.

Addicts like my wife eat the sprouts raw in salads, but I prefer them lightly steamed, sautéed in butter, or tossed into vegetable soup for 5 minutes before serving – or try grinding a handful to add to home-made bread!

from Val Doonican, Entertainer

Colcannon

A very popular dish in Ireland particularly on Fridays, and a 'must' for Halloween. It's very simply made with mashed potatoes and cooked greens, but if possible, curly kale, using about half as much greens as potatoes or as preferred.

potatoes	pepper and salt
greens (preferably curly kale)	milk
butter or margarine	finely chopped onion

Peel and cook the amount of potatoes required. Mash very thoroughly, creaming well with a good knob of butter or margarine, pepper and salt, and a little heated milk.

Cook the kale or greens until tender, drain and chop very finely, add to the mashed potato which has been kept hot. Add a tablespoon or so of very finely chopped onion. Cream all well together and be sure to serve piping hot – with the butter dish near at hand.

from Michael Noakes, Portrait Painter

Mixed vegetables

It might conjure up a picturesque image if I claimed that I gleaned this mouth-watering way of dealing with mixed vegetables from an aged gipsy in a remote corner of Herefordshire. Alas, it would be untrue – but perhaps it is no less romantic to say that my wife often cooks them this way and since I think she's a very good cook, that is a real recommendation.

1 onion	1 tin tomatoes
1 green pepper	butter
a few sticks celery	salt and black pepper
1 clove garlic, crushed	

Peel and slice the onion and fry gently in butter. Add the sliced pepper and celery and the garlic, toss together in the butter for a minute or so, then add the tomatoes. Season. Heat until the mixture is thoroughly hot, but do not over-cook – it is important that the vegetables stay crisp.

This is very good served as a vegetable with a main dish, particularly fish or steak, and it can also be used in the preparation of a shepherd's pie, or steak and kidney pie. For these, use a good flavoursome household dripping collected from the roast instead of butter. Fry the onions and the garlic, then add the meat and fry until it is brown. Add the other vegetables, and cook the mixture in a slow oven until the meat is tender – the slower the cooking the tastier the pie.

Other vegetables can be added – to serve as a vegetable, add olives at the same time as the tomatoes, or for a pie fry mushrooms with the onions and garlic before adding the meat.

from Ted Kotcheff, Film Director

Bulgarian stuffed peppers

To serve 4

4 large sweet peppers	oil
2 medium sized onions	¾ lb. minced beef

½ lb. minced pork
1 tin tomatoes
parsley
bay leaf

salt and freshly ground black
pepper
½ cup cooked rice
paprika

Chop and sauté onions in a little oil until soft. Add beef, and then pork, and cook until lightly browned. Then add tomatoes, parsley and bay, two teaspoons salt and freshly ground black pepper, and continue cooking. Finally add cooked rice and 1 large teaspoon paprika. The mixture should be semi-cooked at this stage.

Remove stalks from peppers and hollow out centres, removing all seeds and pith. Keep stalks and bases to cover peppers when stuffed. Spoon mixture into peppers, not filling too full, cover with stalk bases, place in casserole or saucepan together with any left-over filling and simmer for 1 hour on a low heat.

from The Rt Hon. Lord Shawcross, Q.C. and Company Director

Hot mushroom pie

To serve about 6

1 pastry shell*
1 lb. mushrooms
2 tablesp. butter
2 tablesp. olive oil
1 Spanish onion, finely chopped
1 tablesp. flour

½ pt single cream
1 egg, beaten
2 tablesp. dry sherry
salt and freshly ground black
pepper

Line a pie tin with pastry, fluting the edges. Chill. Prick bottom with a fork and bake blind in a hot oven for about 15 minutes, just long enough to set the crust without browning it. Allow to cool.

Clean and slice the mushrooms and sauté in butter and olive oil with the finely chopped onion until onion is transparent. Stir in flour, and cook, stirring continuously, for 2 minutes.

Combine cream with beaten egg, sherry, salt and freshly ground black pepper to taste. Pour over mushroom mixture into pastry shell and bake in fairly hot oven 400°F. Mark 6 until brown (about 25 mins.).

* Ed. Whatever pastry you usually use for tarts or flans may be used for this recipe, or make a pâte brisée.

from Dulcie Gray, Actress and Writer
Dulcie Gray's tomatoes provençale

For each tomato allow:

1 anchovy fillet	1 dessertsp. oil
olives	salt and pepper
1 small onion	1 tablesp. breadcrumbs
crushed garlic	chopped parsley

Cut the top off the tomato and scoop out the seeds, leaving the solid flesh; using the back of a spoon, rub the rest through a sieve, discarding the seeds.

Slice anchovies and olives. Chop onion well and fry gently in oil with the garlic until brown. Stir sieved tomato and all other ingredients into onion and garlic keeping back some breadcrumbs. Mix well. Stuff the mixture into the tomatoes, sprinkle with remaining breadcrumbs, dot with butter and bake in a well-oiled dish for 25 minutes in a moderate oven 355°F. Mark 4.

from Richard Attenborough, Film Actor and Director
Stuffed aubergines

2 aubergines	1 dessertsp. flour
4 lambs' kidneys	1 teasp. tomato purée
1½ oz. butter	¼ pt stock
2 medium sized onions, finely sliced	1 clove garlic, crushed with ½ teasp. salt

salt and pepper	1 tablesp. grated cheese,
1 bay leaf	preferably Parmesan
½ lb. tomatoes, roughly chopped	1 tablesp. fresh white
2–3 tablesp. salad oil	breadcrumbs

Split aubergines in two length-ways, score round edge and across, salt and leave for 30 minutes to *dégorger* (drain).

Skin the kidneys, cut out cores and cut in half length-ways. Heat a small sauté pan, drop in half the butter and when foaming, put in the kidneys. Brown quickly on all sides, then remove from the pan and keep warm. Lower the heat, add remaining butter and the onions. Cook for 2–3 minutes then draw aside. Stir in the flour, tomato purée and stock and bring to the boil. Add the crushed garlic to the pan with pepper, bay leaf and the kidneys. Cover and simmer gently for about 20 minutes.

Wipe the aubergines dry and sauté rather slowly in 2–3 tablespoons of oil until soft. (*Note:* Aubergines brown very quickly when sautéed. If the flesh is browned before being cooked right through, complete cooking in oven.) Skin the tomatoes, remove the seeds and roughly chop flesh. When the aubergines are tender, scoop out the pulp with a spoon, leaving the skins intact.

Remove bay leaf from the kidneys, add the tomatoes and aubergine pulp and simmer together for 2–3 minutes. Set the aubergine skins in an oven-proof dish, fill with the mixture and dust the tops with the cheese and crumbs. Brown in a quick oven 425°F. Mark 7 for approximately 7 minutes.

from Anita Harris, Singer and Apprentice Cook

Anita's cauliflower soufflé

A very major point to remember: Do not open the oven door to see how the soufflé is cooking until the cooking time is up and then open the door very gently and make sure that your kid brother is not playing Batman within a radius of three

miles, otherwise the draught will make your soufflé end up
with a (to quote a Batman phrase) 'SPLATT ! ! !'

1 large cauliflower	1 oz. flour
½ onion	1 oz. butter
salt, pepper and nutmeg	3 eggs
2 tablesp. Parmesan cheese	

Boil the cauliflower and sliced onion in salted water, remove
stalks and put the flowerets and their stems and the onion
through a sieve or mill. Season with salt, pepper and nutmeg.
Stir in the Parmesan.

Make a white roux with the butter and flour, add the cauliflower and cheese mixture (and if necessary, a little water).
Add the egg yolks, stirring them in one by one. Keep the mixture
warm while you whip the whites of egg and when they are stiff,
fold them into the cauliflower mixture.

Butter a soufflé dish and put in the mixture – it should come
about half-way up so that there is room for it to rise. Place in a
hot oven for 15–20 minutes.

PUDDINGS AND SWEET DISHES

from Nina Bawden, Novelist

Grapes with cream

Even people who don't like puddings find this delicious.

a good bunch of green grapes
double cream
soft brown sugar (not demerara)

Peel *and pip* the grapes, lay them in a flat, fireproof dish and cover thickly with stiff, whipped cream. Keep in refrigerator at least half a day (cold, but not *too* cold or the cream will granulate) and just before serving sprinkle thickly with soft brown sugar (not demerara) and put under a very hot grill until the toffee crust forms. The cream and grapes should be very cold under the sticky crust.

from The Earl of Harewood, Musical Administrator

Peach crème brûlée

fresh sliced peaches
double cream
soft brown sugar

Three-quarters fill a shallow dish with the sliced peaches. Cover with thickly whipped cream. Chill well. Cover with $\frac{1}{4}$ inch thick layer of soft brown sugar. Chill again. At the last moment, place the dish under a very hot grill, caramelize the sugar and serve at once.

from Rosalie Crutchley, Actress
Orange syllabub

This is a very quick and easy sweet and has a subtle and sophisticated taste to end a supper.

2½ small oranges	2 oz. caster sugar
½ lemon	½ pt double cream

Finely grate rind from 1 orange into mixing basin. Squeeze
juice of oranges and lemon, strain and add to rind. Add sugar
and stir until dissolved. Pour in cream and whisk until mixture
is thick. Pour into individual glasses or small pots and chill until
ready to serve.

from Shirley Conran, Designer, Writer, Harassed Hostess
Sultry grapefruit mousse

I invented this recipe myself in desperation. It is very good
after a rich meal such as curry or duck.

1 19 oz. tin grapefruit juice	grated rind and juice of 1 lemon
1 oz. powdered gelatine	whites of 4 eggs, well whipped
a little sugar if using	small ctn double cream, well
unsweetened grapefruit juice	whipped

Melt gelatine in 2 tablespoons boiling water, sieve it so there are no
lumps and mix with grapefruit juice (to which sugar has been
added if required) and lemon juice. Stir and leave in refrigerator
until it starts to gel. (If you leave it until it is set hard, then beat
the resulting jelly until you have got it to some form of frothy
state.)

Add well whipped egg whites and whip together. Refrigerate
for at least 1 hour. Pour into a pretty container: I use a 19th-
century celery glass, or individual silver goblets. Top with
whipped cream and a sprinkling of grated lemon peel.

from Stevie Smith, Poet
Junket

1 pt Jersey milk	nutmeg
2 teasp. rennet	1 tablesp. brandy (or whisky)
sugar	Devonshire cream

Warm milk to blood heat, add rennet and sugar to taste. Pour into a cold glass dish and when set and quite cold, grate nutmeg over and add 1 tablespoon of brandy or whisky. Serve with Devonshire cream.

from David Steel, M.P., Broadcaster and Journalist
Children's 'bana' pudding

For each child:

1 chopped banana	1 dessertsp. sugar
1 raw egg	1 tablesp. cream (optional)
1 cup milk	

Put all ingredients into liquidizer. Press the button until smoothly mixed. Pour into dish and serve.

from Dilys Powell, Author and Film Critic
Chocolate mousse

Since I have no time, no inclination, and, good heavens, positively no talent for cooking I send a recipe for something which doesn't *need* to be cooked. It isn't exactly cheap, but at least it saves work and that other commodity which nowadays nobody seems to possess – leisure.

To serve 6–8

4 oz. bitter chocolate	1 oz. softened butter
4 eggs	juice of ½ orange

Break chocolate into squares and put in low oven – or over hot water – to melt. When chocolate is soft, stir in 4 well-beaten egg-yolks, and then add the softened butter and orange juice. Beat the egg-whites to a froth and fold into the chocolate mixture. Pour into little pots, glasses or coffee cups and put in refrigerator to set.

from Pamela Hansford Johnson, Writer

Coffee russe

This is really a party dish, and is so rich that the quantities given are enough for 4–5 people. They can be doubled for a greater number.

To serve 4–5

3 oz. butter	3 tablesp. very hot, strong coffee
3 oz. caster sugar	(a spoonful of coffee essence
yolks of 3 eggs	may be added if liked)
½ oz. gelatine	sponge fingers

Line a mould with the sponge fingers, sides only. Cream together until very soft, butter and sugar, beat in yolks of eggs. Melt gelatine in coffee and beat into the mixture. Pour into mould and allow to set overnight.

from Benjamin Britten, Composer
Dark treacle jelly

4 tablesp. dark treacle   lemon juice to taste
1 pkt (½ oz.) gelatine   1 tablesp. sugar (optional)

Dissolve gelatine in a little water. Melt all ingredients together
in a saucepan, make up to 1 pt with water. Stir well, turn into a
wetted mould and leave to set.

from Hayley Mills, Actress
Prune bombe

To serve 6

1 lb. best prunes   1½ pts ice-cream, vanilla and
twist of lemon peel   coffee
¼ teasp. powdered cinnamon   4 whites of egg
¼ pt brandy or Jamaican rum   1 dessertsp. caster sugar

Bring prunes to boil in just enough water to cover, with the
lemon peel and cinnamon, and boil gently for 5 minutes to
plump them slightly. Pour off the water, pour on the rum or

brandy and leave to soak overnight. Next day, simmer them gently in the liquor in which they have soaked for ½ hour.

Preheat oven to 450°F. Mark 8, hot. Put half ice-cream into a large oven-glass casserole, add prunes, cover with remaining ice-cream, top with stiffly beaten egg whites into which caster sugar has been folded. Pop back into oven for 5–10 minutes to brown the meringue. Serve at once.

from Cleo Laine, Singer

Gooseberry fool

As I'm always on a diet and resent making puddings for the family, I don't go in for the grand, sugary delight that takes so much time – and also tempts you, as you have to taste. This pudding is quite delicious and as it's not time consuming, dieters can somehow ignore it.

1 can gooseberries	cream
similar quantity of thick custard	granulated sugar (optional)

Liquidize the gooseberries, add the custard and cream to taste. Let this set in a cool place and serve with a sprinkling of granulated sugar if desired.

Other fruits, tinned or fresh, can be experimented with – I suggest on the family first.

from Sir Compton Mackenzie, Author

Peach and orange salad

This is a delicious combination.

to every 3 peaches 1 large orange	orange juice
caster sugar	orange curaçao (optional)

Slice peaches very thinly. Cut oranges transversely and prise sections out. Start filling dish with a layer of orange, followed by three layers of peaches, a good sprinkling of caster sugar and orange juice. Continue so until dish is filled, according to amount required.

If really fresh peaches are used, no liqueur is necessary, but a touch of orange curaçao may be used.

from Dorothy Tutin, Actress
Boodles pudding

This recipe is simple and easy and can be done before the hurly-burly of a dinner party. It can also make up for the disaster of any middle course!

8 dry sponge cakes   1 pt thick cream
2 lemons   sugar
4 oranges

Grate the rind of 2 oranges and 1 lemon. Squeeze the juice of all the fruit and strain it. Sweeten to taste and add the cream, slightly whipped.

Fill a soufflé dish with the sponge cakes cut in half and pour the fruit cream over them. Place in refrigerator for several hours.

from Cliff Michelmore, Television Commentator
Dutch apple tart

short crust pastry   brown sugar
cooking apples (dessert apples   mixed spice
   may also be used)   sultanas

For the glaze: 1 tablesp. apricot jam
1 tablesp. redcurrant jelly

Line an open tart dish with the pastry. Make an apple purée, sweeten it with brown sugar and add a little ground mixed spice and some sultanas, to taste. Cool, and fill the tart. Cover with thin overlapping slices of raw apple and bake in a fairly hot oven 400°F. Mark 6 about ½ hour or until pastry is cooked. Remove from oven and glaze.

To make the glaze: put 1 tablesp. of water in a saucepan with the redcurrant jelly and apricot jam and beat, stirring constantly until syrupy. Brush this over the apple slices with a pastry brush.

Can be eaten hot or cold.

from Oswald Mair, Executive Chef, London Hilton

American blueberry pie

This is the traditional pie which has become almost a national dish in America. It is made on a fireproof plate, and may be made with a crust underneath the fruit or simply on top.

1 lb. blueberries   1 oz. butter or margarine
4 oz. sugar, or more if liked   1 oz. sugar
1 tablesp. lemon juice   pinch of salt
For the pastry: 1 egg yolk
8 oz. plain flour   water to mix
¼ oz. baking powder
or
8 oz. self-raising flour

Rub in fat, flour, salt and sugar. Add egg yolk, mix in a little water until pastry is of rollable consistency. Roll out and line a 9-inch plate with half. Fill with blueberries, sprinkle with sugar and lemon juice. Roll out rest of pastry and cover pie. Bake in a hot oven 450°F. Mark 8 for about ½ hour or until crust is brown.

from Dr Roy Strong, Director of the National Portrait
Gallery

Charlotte basque

To produce a splendid, mouth-watering pudding is to me the
test of a really good cook or hostess. Few take the trouble these
days.

If you decide to cook a good pudding, plan your other courses
around it. Make the main course a plain roast with herbs or
garlic (no complicated sauces) and green vegetables (no potatoes
or root vegetables) followed by a salad. Then have a short
interval and produce for admiration, contemplation and
joyous consumption your pudding. Here is a recipe for one of
my favourites which I love to cook. Every mouthful is a taste
experience.

To serve 6–8

3 oz. granulated sugar	¼ teasp. almond extract
4 large egg yolks	2 tablesp. rum, kirsch, cognac or
1 teasp. vanilla extract	cointreau
1 teasp. cornflour	¼ pt water
¾ pt milk	¼ pt orange liqueur
small bar plain chocolate	about 24 sponge fingers
¼ lb. unsalted butter	½ pt double cream
3 oz. ground almonds	

Start by making a *crème anglaise*: beat together the egg yolks
and sugar until the mixture is a pale yellow. Add vanilla and
beat in cornflour. Bring the milk to the boil with 3 oz. of the
chocolate broken up in it and melted. Continue to beat the
yolks, gradually pouring in the boiling milk in a thin stream.
Pour mixture into a clean saucepan and stir with a wooden
spatula or spoon over a low heat. Do *not* allow to come to
simmering point and when the custard coats the spoon with a
thin, creamy lather, remove. Continue stirring a minute or so.

Pour into a basin, allow to cool and put into refrigerator until cold.

Cream butter and ground almonds in a large mixing bowl. Gradually beat in the cold *crème anglaise*, almond extract, liqueur or rum. Put a round of greaseproof paper in the bottom of the mould or basin. Place water and orange liqueur in a soup plate and dip in the sponge fingers. As you dip them, line the mould with them, firstly the bottom then the sides. When you have finished doing this, pour in some of the mixture, then a layer of the dipped sponge fingers, and so on to the top. Place in the refrigerator.

Remove when needed and tip out on to a plate. Whip double cream and place in a forcing bag. Decorate pudding. Grate a little of the remaining plain chocolate over it if you wish.

from Adrian Jardine, Olympic Sailing Medallist

Fruit pancakes

This is a very tasty dish that can be served any time at sea even in the worst conditions. Prepare one at home before the start of a trip.

10–12 thin pancakes (use ordinary recipe)
caster sugar

8 oz. apple sauce or stewed rhubarb (well strained)

Take one pancake and spread with apple sauce or rhubarb. Put second pancake on top. Spread this one in same way, put third pancake on top. Continue in this way until all pancakes are used up. Trim edges and sprinkle top pancake with caster sugar. Serve cold, cut into wedges, with cream. Other fruit purées can be used if preferred.

from Mrs Mary Wilson
Queen of puddings

To serve 4

1 oz. butter
1 pt milk
3 oz. breadcrumbs
2 oz. sugar

raspberry jam
1½ oz. caster sugar
2 eggs

Butter a pie-dish. Soak the breadcrumbs in the milk. Add the 2 oz. sugar and the egg yolks and mix well. Pour into the pie-dish and bake in a moderate oven 380°F. Mark 5 till set. Cool slightly and spread with jam. Whisk the whites of eggs and the caster sugar until stiff and pile on top of the pudding. Bake again in a slow oven 240°F. Mark ¼ until the meringue is brown. Serve hot.

from The Very Rev. Dr Immanuel Jacobowitz, Chief Rabbi
Apple strudel

½ lb. flour
pinch salt
1 small egg
2 tablesp. olive oil
about ¼ pt warm water
1 lb. apples

1 tablesp. breadcrumbs
2 oz. margarine
a few almonds
3 tablesp. currants
brown sugar
lemon juice

Sieve flour and salt into a bowl; beat egg, add oil and pour into middle of flour together with a little *warm* water. Do not put all the water in to start with; it depends on the size of the egg and dryness of the flour how much will be needed. Mix with a fork and then knead with the hand very thoroughly to a soft, pliable dough that does not stick to the hands or bowl. Put on the pastry board, cover with a warm basin and leave for ½ hour. Then, lay a clean cloth on the working surface, sprinkle it with flour, put the pastry in the middle, roll it out and pull it with the hands until it is almost thin enough to see through.

Peel the apples, cut into very thin slices, brown the bread-crumbs in a little margarine, mix them with the apples, cleaned currants and chopped almonds. Sweeten with brown sugar and flavour with lemon juice. Spread over the pastry and sprinkle with a little melted margarine. Raise one side of the cloth and roll the pastry and apple like a 'roly-poly'. Form into a crescent, place on a greased baking sheet, brush over with the remaining margarine, and bake for about 40 minutes. Start in a hot oven 445°F. Mark 8 and when lightly browned reduce to moderate 380°F. Mark 5.

This recipe comes from Florence Greenberg's *Jewish Cookery Book*.

from Tommy Steele, Actor

Bread and butter pudding (1)

His mother makes it this way.

To serve 4

12 slices of bread	½ teasp. vanilla extract
butter	2 eggs
about 2 tablesp. raisins	rind of 1 lemon, coarsely grated
½ pt milk	rind of 1 orange, coarsely grated

Trim the crusts from the bread, butter the slices and cut each slice in half. Place the bread slices in a well-buttered baking dish and scatter a few raisins between each layer.

Warm the milk, add the vanilla. Separate the eggs, and whisk yolks with the vanilla-flavoured milk. Whisk whites until stiff and fold into the egg and milk mixture. Pour the mixture over the bread, sprinkle with half the grated lemon and orange rind, and bake in a moderate oven 380°F Mark 5 for about 40 minutes or until pudding is set and golden brown. Use remainder of lemon and orange rind to decorate pudding, and serve hot.

from Michael Flanders, Actor and Writer

Bread and butter pudding (2)

Served hot, this dish is a great comfort in time of trouble. It is also said to be delicious cold but we never have any left over.

To serve 4 polite people or 2 greedy ones

4 slices white bread	⅔ pt milk
butter	2 oz. sugar
pineapple or apricot jam	nutmeg
about 2 oz. sultanas	small triangles of dry bread
3 large eggs	

Butter the bread and make 2 pineapple or apricot jam sand-wiches. Remove crusts, cut into small cubes and place in a fire-proof dish. Sprinkle the sultanas over.

Cover with the eggs, milk, sugar and a little freshly grated nutmeg, well beaten together. Decorate all over with small triangles of dry bread dipped in melted butter.

Bake in warm oven 335°F. Mark 3 for 45 minutes or until brown and set. Serve. Sleep.

from Mary Kelly, Writer
Mrs Tribe's steamed pudding

Very nice, extra light, easy to make, never fails.

To serve 2–3

3 oz. butter (unsalted creams best)
2 tablesp. sugar
1 level tablesp. golden syrup
2 teasp. marmalade
1 egg

2 rounded tablesp. self-raising flour
dried fruit as liked (raisins are good – a small handful)
a little milk if necessary

Cream butter and sugar, add syrup and marmalade, beat well. Sieve in 1 tablespoon of the flour and beat. Add the egg and beat. Then add the rest of the flour and the dried fruit. Beat well. The mixture should drop in soft, ragged lumps from the spoon. If too dry add milk.

Put in a greased basin, cover well and steam for at least 2 hours. Makes 3 good or 2 large helpings.

CAKES

from William MacQuitty, Film Producer, Author, Photographer

Irish potato cakes

The Irish struggled to make these during the Troubles when they were thrown out of their cottages or had the thatched roofs burnt over their heads. In those days, they just beat together cooked potatoes and buttermilk, but for more affluent English tea-tables:

1 lb. potatoes	1 egg
1 oz. butter	flour (about 2 tablesp.)

Sieve or mash potatoes with the butter and egg to make a smooth, stiff paste. Form with flour into flat cakes about ¾ inch thick. Cook on griddle or frying pan until golden brown on both sides. Serve hot, split and spread liberally with butter and honey.

from Harry Secombe, Singer and Comedian

Welsh cakes

This is one of Mrs Secombe's specialities.

1 lb. self-raising flour	4 oz. caster sugar
5 oz. lard	3 oz. sultanas
5 oz. butter	3 oz. currants
pinch of salt	2 eggs

Rub fat into flour, add salt, sugar and fruit and mix together. Make a well in the mixture and add the two beaten eggs and a little warm water if necessary. Turn out on to a floured board and knead lightly. Roll the mixture out to $\frac{1}{4}$ inch thickness and cut out with a round, fluted cutter. Place on a greased hot-plate or griddle. Cook at moderate heat until golden brown on both sides.

from Diana Rigg, Actress
Flapjack

An old family recipe – all men and children adore it.

6 oz. butter	1 heaped tablesp. golden syrup
6 tablesp. sugar	salt
2 oz. lard	20 *heaped* tablesp. Quaker Oats

Cream butter and sugar. Beat in other ingredients. Pat into flat tins (about ½ inch deep) with back of buttered wooden spoon. Bake ten minutes in hot oven 425°F. Mark 7 until pale golden brown. When half cold, cut into oblong biscuits.

from Mia Farrow, Actress
Chocolate bon bon cookies

1 cup butter	¼ teasp. salt
½ cup sugar	2 ctns (8 oz. each) whole candied
1 teasp. vanilla	cherries
1 egg	a little sugar
6 oz. grated chocolate	a little milk
3 cups flour, sifted	

Cream butter and sugar and beat till fluffy. Add vanilla and egg and beat again till well mixed. Blend in the grated chocolate. Stir in the flour and salt.

Take small pieces of the dough and put a cherry in the centre; roll between palms of hands into balls covering the cherry. Place on baking sheets and refrigerate 15 minutes. Then bake in a moderate oven 380°F. Mark 5 till firm – 12 minutes. When cool, dip into a glaze of sugar mixed with milk. Garnish as desired.

from Terry Wogan, Disc-Jockey

Pavlova cake

If our hero has a fault, it can only be that his life revolves around his stomach. His lovely wife, Helen, must shoulder some of the blame for this, she being a cook of the first water. Our boy has an easy mastery over the difficult culinary arts, such as the boiling of eggs and the grilling of rashers. Instant mashed potato is child's play to him. The simpler little things he leaves to Helen, such as:

3 egg whites
pinch of salt
1 cup caster sugar
1 teasp. vinegar

1 teasp. cornflour
2 bananas
½ pt double cream

Beat egg whites until stiff with pinch of salt. Beat in half the sugar and *fold* in remainder. Fold in vinegar and cornflour.

Line an 8-inch sandwich tin with greaseproof paper and fold in the mixture. Bake in centre of a slow oven 300°F. Mark 1–2 for ½ hour, then very slow 250°F. Mark ¼–½ for ¾ hour. Allow to cool, turn upside down onto a plate, decorate with bananas and whipped cream.

from Stirling Moss, former Racing Driver, Company Director

Coffee meringue cake

4 egg whites
½ lb. caster sugar
For the butter cream:
4 oz. sugar
½ gill water
4 egg yolks

¾ lb. unsalted butter
coffee essence
For the decoration:
browned almonds, finely chopped
coffee dragées

Have ready 3 baking sheets lined with bakewell paper. Set oven at slow 265°–290°F. Mark ½–1. Prepare the meringue: whisk egg whites stiffly, add 1 teasp. sugar and whisk again until quite stiff, then fold in the rest of the sugar. Spread or pipe the mixture into thin rounds 8–9 inches in diameter on the prepared baking tins. Bake until dry and crisp (about 50–60 minutes).

Meanwhile prepare the butter cream. Dissolve the sugar in the water, boil 'to the thread', that is, until it is sticky, and pour on to the egg yolks. Whisk until thick. Cream the butter and beat in the egg mousse by degrees. Flavour with the coffee essence.

When the meringue rounds are quite cold, spread with the butter cream and shape it into a cake. Spread the top and sides with the same cream and cover with the browned almonds. Decorate with the dragées.

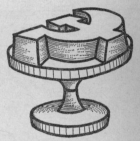

from Gillian Tindall, Novelist and Journalist

Russian cheesecake

On the whole I am not a recipe user, so I am never sure how I make anything when I'm doing it, but I *think* this is how I make it.

about 1 lb. curd cheese (Sainsburys have a good, cheap one, or you can spend hours making your own. I don't)

2–3 oz. white sugar, depending on how sweet-toothed your family are

handful of raisins or sultanas

few drops vanilla essence (but if
you've forgotten to buy it it
isn't essential)
Some people like a few drops
lemon juice in it too

spoonful cream
1 egg
butter
sour cream or home-made
yoghourt

Put the cheese in a bowl, add the sugar, sultanas or raisins, vanilla, lemon juice if used, and cream. Mix well. Beat the egg and add it to the mixture. Mix again. (For some mysterious reason if you make double quantity, you don't need twice as much egg – it becomes too runny.)

Put mixture into a buttered oven dish (small and deep if you want a pudding, bigger and shallower if you have more of a cake in mind). Dot top with not too much butter and sprinkle with sugar. Bake in a medium oven 355°F. Mark 4 till done (20–30 minutes according to taste). Eat at once, while it's not too firmly set, with sour cream, like the Russians; or eat later, colder and firmer – 'like me' says my husband.

Or try it with *home-made yoghourt*: not a joke but just much nicer than the bought sort. Thus:

Home-made yoghourt

milk
spoonful live yoghourt

cream, fresh or tinned

Boil milk. Pour into bowl, preferably earthenware. Put to cool, stirring at intervals so that no thick skin forms. When luke-warm add a spoonful left over from the last lot (start the cycle by buying one expensive 'live' yoghourt from a Health Food store). You can also add a bit of cream, real or tinned. Cover. Put to set for a few hours in a warm place (e.g. greenhouse, hot cupboard, pre-warmed oven) but not too hot or the ferment will pathetically die. When set, i.e. soft but firm, transfer to fridge.

You do not need thermos, special bowls, containers, thermometers or any of the other kit that people like to use.

from Jimmy Young, Disc-Jockey and Singer
Mrs Hyde's pineapple delights

8 oz. short crust pastry
8 oz. tin pineapple chunks,
   drained and chopped finely
a little of the pineapple juice
2 oz. margarine

2 oz. sugar
1 egg
8 oz. dessicated coconut
2 drops almond essence

Roll out the pastry thinly and line two dozen individual cake tins with it after greasing them well. Into each patty case put a little chopped pineapple.

Melt margarine and put in a basin. Beat in egg and sugar and the dessicated coconut. Mix well, then add almond essence and a little pineapple juice to make a good dropping consistency. Put a teaspoon of the mixture into each pastry case. Bake for 15 minutes in a moderately hot oven 380°F. Mark 5.

This recipe has appeared in *The Third Jimmy Young Cook Book*, a B.B.C. publication.

from Wilfrid Pickles, Actor
Christmas cake

¾ lb. currants
1¼ lb. seedless raisins
¾ lb. sultanas
¼ lb. mixed candied peel
6 oz. glacé cherries
¼ lb. ground almonds
1 lb. self-raising flour
pinch salt
½ lb. butter or margarine

½ lb. brown sugar
6 eggs
3 tablesp. rum
For decoration:
caster sugar
glacé cherries
angelica
almonds

Clean, dry and remove any stalks from dried fruit. Chop the raisins and mixed candied peel. Halve the glacé cherries and rub lightly in flour. Sieve flour and salt on piece of kitchen paper. Cream fat and sugar together until light and fluffy. Beat eggs together and add gradually to creamed mixture, beating well.

If mixture curdles add a little of sifted flour. Stir in dried fruit, mixed peel, cherries and ground almonds, then mix in rest of flour. Stir in rum.

Turn mixture into prepared 9-inch tin. To prepare tin, grease and line with round of brown paper and two rounds of greaseproof paper in bottom, and double thickness strip of greaseproof paper round sides. Grease lining.

Hollow out centre of cake mixture slightly with wooden spoon to make flat top for icing when cooked. Tie double thickness of brown paper round outside of tin and put cake in prepared moderately hot oven 335°F. Mark 3. Turn oven down to low 290°F. Mark 1 after 1 hour and continue cooking for about another 3 hours, or until a warmed skewer or steel knitting needle comes out clean when pushed through centre of cake. Allow to cool slightly in tin before turning out on wire rack and removing paper. When cold, cover top with almond paste and mark into a pattern with back of knife-blade or skewer. Brown top gently in moderate oven or under grill. Sprinkle with caster sugar and decorate with halved glacé cherries, blanched almonds and angelica.

MISCELLANEOUS

from Yehudi Menuhin, Violinist

Birchermuesli

This Swiss recipe is particularly delicious in its summer form which I have given here, but can equally well be eaten all the year round in a less exciting style, substituting the berries by 3 grated apples. It can be served as a breakfast dish or as a dessert, instead of fresh fruit. One must naturally use one's judgement with regard to the amount of sugar or the thickness of the cream, both of these depending upon the particular quality and choice of fruit used. The Swiss add a lovely almond purée which can be bought in Switzerland in tins and is called 'Nuxo'. The recipe was invented by the famous vegetarian doctor, Bircher, and literally means 'Bircher porridge'. It is as healthy as it is delicious.

To serve 4

2 level tablesp. precooked
  oatflakes
2 tablesp. brown sugar
juice of ½ lemon
½ banana (mashed)
2 tablesp. thin cream (or 1
  thick)

1 jar yoghourt
juice of 2 oranges
½ grated apple
berries in season (strawberries,
  raspberries, blueberries)
finely chopped ground almonds

Mix the oatflakes, sugar, lemon juice, banana and cream and blend well. Add yoghourt, orange juice and grated apple immediately to prevent it browning. Wash about 1 lb. of whatever berries are in season and hull them. Mash three-quarters of them and add to the mixture. Decorate with the remaining whole fruit, sprinkle with the almonds, chill slightly and serve either in a glass bowl or in individual glass ice-cream dishes.

from the Rt Hon. Jeremy Thorpe, Leader of the Liberal Party

Camembert ice savoury

To serve 6

1 lb. camembert cheese
equal quantity of cream
cayenne pepper

grated Parmesan cheese
paprika

Mix the camembert with the cream and a little cayenne pepper. Freeze. Cut into fingers. Roll in grated Parmesan cheese and decorate with paprika. Serve with hot biscuits and butter.

from Richard Hamilton, Painter

Crisp sandwich

I'm not a great cook but that is because I'm not a great reader: as I often tell Rita, 'If you can read you can cook'. The following recipe was given to me verbally by a Geordie student in Newcastle University. It tastes better than it sounds.

2 slices of bread (preferably wax
    wrapped, ready sliced)

butter or margarine
potato crisps

Butter the slices of bread thinly on one side only (margarine may be used as an economic alternative). Place one slice on a table, butter side up, and spread a layer of potato crisps evenly over the bread. Take the second slice and press it firmly, butter side down, on to the crisps.

Smith's Golden Wonder or Tudor crisps may be used though Marks and Spencer's are recommended. If the packet has been open for some days put them into a warm oven for a few minutes to crispen them up. As a variation, try chips (warm) treated in the same way.

from Ron Moody, Actor, Writer of Musicals
Sauce vinaigrette

I know absolutely nothing about cooking, except I prefer my own sauce vinaigrette to anybody else's, particularly with avocado pears. I use a lot of vinegar, half the amount of oil, salt and pepper to taste and a little mustard. *But the real touch is to take a dice or two of an onion and chop it into tiny pieces.* Mix it all together and drop it on half an avocado (the bit without the stone) and eat it all up.

Incidentally, for tossed green salad, I think that the vinaigrette should be simpler, without mustard or onion but with a little sugar. (Italian restaurants put in too much oil, and French, too much mustard.)

from Bernard Miles, Actor-Manager and Theatrical Jack-of-all-Trades
Tea and kippers

Take 2 Rothesay kippers (or even 3) and grill until the flesh begins to curl away from the skin. Serve with brown bread and butter and tea, made in a brown crock tea-pot – two heaped teaspoons per person.

Making tea is not so simple. Warm both pot and cup. Mash the tea with just sufficient water to cover it. Leave for two minutes. Then fill the pot. I take it for granted every household has a tea-cosy.

The meal should preferably be taken at a deal table without table-cloth, in front of a log fire and after a hard walk in the winter sunshine.

I got this from my mother who got it from her grandmother.

from Max Bygraves, Entertainer
Tea

I don't worry too much about food but I consider a good cup of tea essential. It's amazing how many people in this tea-drinking country do not know how to make a good cup of tea. I pass on the recipe, which I feel is of far more benefit to me than food.

Bring freshly drawn water to a full rolling boil (reheated water has a flat taste). Use a teapot, preheat it and dry it. Put in one teaspoon of tea per cup plus 'one for the pot': a tea-bag is equivalent to one teaspoon of tea. Steep the tea to the strength you prefer: 3–5 minutes. After brewing, decant into a serving pot: for weaker tea, add hot water to the cup when serving.

Don't judge the strength of tea by its colour – delicate teas may produce a dark brew – strong teas a light brew, depending on the blend of tea.

from Colin Davis, Musician
How to cook Sainsbury's long grain rice

Soak the rice for as many hours as you can spare in heavily salted water. Drain and put it into fiercely boiling water. Watch over it and when it is half cooked, take it off the gas and strain it through a colander or sieve. To complete the cooking, put about $\frac{1}{4}$ inch of water in the bottom of a saucepan with a large knob of butter. When the butter has melted, pour half the liquid into a cup. Pile the rice back into the saucepan in the shape of a pyramid. Put it on a medium gas and pour the liquid from the cup over the pyramid of rice. Put the lid on and when steam issues from the saucepan, lower the gas, wrap the saucepan lid in an old towel or tea-cloth and brew the rice over a very low gas. If it is left long enough, it will form a crust at the bottom of the saucepan and the rest of the rice should be quite separate, dry and buttered.

from Edna O'Brien, Author
Soul bread

With love to Aretha Franklin.

2 lb. brown flour	8 oz. butter
1 lb. white flour	1 tablesp. honey
2 teasp. bicarbonate of soda	sour milk (unpasteurized)
1 teasp. salt	

Sieve white flour, salt and bicarbonate. Crumble butter into it. Add the brown flour, then moisten with honey and sour milk. Knead it well with the hands. It should be firm but slippery. Bake in a hot oven 425°F. Mark 7 for 1 hour.

from Alison Uttley, Author
Damson cheese

Damson cheese was a delicacy of Victorian and Georgian days, and Parson Woodruffe mentions it in his diary of the eighteenth century. It has no connection with cheese or any savoury dish; it is purely a confection for the tea-table. Old ladies took presents of damson cheese when they went out to tea, a contribution to a frugal household welcomed with cries of delight. The cheese was contained in a small cut-glass dish or a pretty porcelain bowl, with flowers or an incised pattern of crosses round the sides. I never saw an ordinary jam pot with damson cheese. It was a special gift which had an element of charm and mystery for young people who enjoyed the sharp, sweet taste as they ate it with thin bread and butter.

Most people had a few damson trees in their gardens, half-wild and straggling. We had several trees growing near walls, as a shade, close to the orchard walls or the pig-cote garden where the little pigs danced and dug their noses. The trees dropped their fruit, but we did not bother to pick the fruit except for damson cheese, and a pie now and then. The fruit was rather bitter but it made good preserve which everybody liked. So we took our pots to friends when we paid a visit.

To make: pick the damsons and remove the stalks and wash the fruit well in spring water. Simmer in a brass or copper preserving pan, until the fruit is soft, stirring all the time. Sieve the fruit, remove stones, weigh the pulp and return it to the pan with its juice and ½ lb. sugar to 1 lb. pulp. Simmer for 2 hours and skim. Boil quickly, stirring, until the pulp looks firm and stiff. Pour into a collection of little pots or jars, as decorative and pretty as you possess. Leave to set and get cold.

The damson cheese keeps for a year or two and never loses its delicacy and charm.

from Fred Streeter, Gardener, Radio and Television Personality

Hints

APPLE TART: use Cox's Orange Pippins – they are as excellent cooked as raw.

A CHRISTMAS DESSERT: get some white currants, string them in layers in a basin, cover each layer with sugar until the crown of the basin is reached. Keep covered, and when solid, cut out in slices.

SPINACH: when cooking spinach, add a few leaves of French sorrel grown from seed. It greatly improves the flavour.

JERUSALEM ARTICHOKES: to get the real flavour from these, slice them and fry instead of boiling, which does away with the smoky flavour.

INDEX OF CONTRIBUTORS

INDEX OF FOODS

More about Penguins

Penguinews, which appears every month, contains details of all the new books issued by Penguins as they are published. From time to time it is supplemented by *Penguins in Print*, which is a complete list of all available books published by Penguins. (There are well over three thousand of these.)

A specimen copy of *Penguinews* will be sent to you free on request, and you can become a subscriber for the price of the postage. For a year's issues (including the complete lists) please send 30p if you live in the United Kingdom, or 60p if you live elsewhere. Just write to Dept EP, Penguin Books Ltd, Harmondsworth, Middlesex, enclosing a cheque or postal order, and your name will be added to the mailing list.

Note: *Penguinews* and *Penguins in Print* are not available in the U.S.A. or Canada

a Penguin Handbook

The Philosopher in the Kitchen

Jean-Anthelme Brillat-Savarin

'Whoever says "truffles" utters a great word which arouses erotic and gastronomic memories among the skirted sex, and memories gastronomic and erotic among the bearded sex.

'This dual distinction is due to the fact that the noble tuber is not only considered delicious to the taste, but is also believed to foster powers the exercise of which is extremely pleasurable.'

'"Rejoice, my dear," I said one day to Madame de V—; "a loom has just been shown to the Society for Encouragement on which it will be possible to manufacture superb lace for practically nothing." '"Why," the lady replied, with an air of supreme indifference, "if lace were cheap, do you think anybody would want to wear such rubbish?"'

Jean-Anthelme Brillat-Savarin (1755–1826), Mayor of Belley, cousin of Madame Récamier, Chevalier de l'Empire, author of a history of duelling and of a number of racy stories (unfortunately lost), whose sister died in her hundredth year having just finished a good meal and shouting loudly for her dessert, is now best known for his *Physiologie du Goût*, here brilliantly translated as *The Philosopher in the Kitchen*, which was first published in December 1825. The work has a timeless appeal – being wise, witty and anecdotal, containing some of the best recipes for food and some of the most satisfactory observations on life.

a Penguin Special

Poverty: The Forgotten Englishman

Ken Coates and Richard Silburn

Is poverty in Britain a thing of the past? Too many of our countrymen regularly do without the minimum considered necessary for a healthy diet; they live in houses that are overcrowded, insanitary and ludicrously expensive to keep warm and comfortable; their children attend schools in which teaching is a near impossibility.

Ken Coates and Richard Silburn look again at what is meant by the word 'poverty'. They conclude that vast numbers of Englishmen, living in slums throughout the country, are, for most of their lives, living in acute poverty. What this actually involves is spelled out by means of a detailed survey of one slum: St Ann's in Nottingham, which is typical of hundreds of such districts.

The book continues with a study of welfare services and why they fail to alleviate or remove poverty. Finally there is an analysis of the frequent failure of slum-clearance schemes and a discussion of new alternatives.

This disturbing Penguin Special attacks a problem – the problem of modern urban poverty – which western society has neglected, is neglecting, but will only go on neglecting at its peril.

a Penguin Special

On Our Conscience
The Plight of the Elderly

Jack Shaw

On Our Conscience is a journalist's graphic report on the
pitiable fate of many old people in our cities.

That the facts came to light in the course of a newspaper
inquiry in Sheffield is no special disgrace to Sheffield.
That city, as it happens, has done as much to clear slums
and provide old folks' homes, geriatric beds, and housing
for the elderly as most comparable cities. Welfare
services, too, are good, though not good enough to cope
with a period when family ties are slackening, relations
lose touch, neighbours move away, and increasingly the
old find themselves stranded.

Hence each year, in the Coroners' Courts, more and more
cases of starvation among the old are recorded as death
from 'self-neglect'.

One horrifying case leads on to another in Jack Shaw's
account of a newspaper campaign which uncovered more
than 1300 examples of old people living neglected, lonely
and miserable lives in the heart of a thriving city. And
in conclusion he suggests the kind of remedies needed
for a social sore which is even more extensive in other
cities in Britain.

a Penguin Special

Civil Liberty
The N.C.C.L. Guide

Anna Coote

No constitution or charter protects British rights. At the mercy of any piece of hasty or prejudiced legislation, they must be upheld in every generation.

Do you possess the 'eternal vigilance' required to safeguard liberty? Do you know, for instance, what your rights are if you are arrested; if you want to hold a meeting or a lottery; to demonstrate in public or vote or strike; to eject an unwelcome visitor or evict a tenant; to adopt a baby or get a divorce; to be educated or obtain a council house or a supplementary benefit; to park your car or sue your dentist?

If you are unsure, this Penguin Special will supply the answers. You will find detailed here all those questions of liberty, justice and human rights about which most men in the street are ignorant or, at best, doubtful. In effect this well ordered and useful guide distils the long experience of the National Council of Civil Liberties in standing up (both politically and through case-work) for 'us' against 'them'.